Get Started With Wire Jewelry

Compiled by Julia Gerlach

Printed in the United States of America

05 06 07 08 09 10 11 12 13 14 10 9 8 7 6 5 4 3 2 1

Publisher's Cataloging-In-Publication Data
(Prepared by The Donohue Group, Inc.)

Get started with wire jewelry / compiled by Julia Gerlach.

   p. : ill. ; cm.
   ISBN: 0-87116-234-2

1. Jewelry making. 2. Wire craft. I. Gerlach, Julia. II. Title.

TT212 .G48 2005
745.594/2

Managing art director: Lisa Bergman
Book layout: Sabine Beaupré
Photographers: Bill Zuback and Jim Forbes
Project editors: Julia Gerlach, Cheryl Phelan

Acknowledgements: Mindy Brooks, Terri Field, Lora Groszkiewicz, Kellie Jaeger, Carrie Jebe, Diane Jolie, Patti Keipe, Alice Korach, Tonya Limberg, Debbie Nishihara, Pam O'Connor, Carole Ross, Candice St. Jacques, Maureen Schimmel, Lisa Schroeder, Terri Torbeck, Elizabeth Weber, Lesley Weiss

CONTENTS

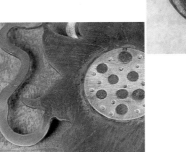

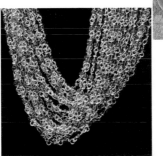

WORKING WITH WIRE

Though rather unassuming, wire and metal can be a jewelry-maker's best friend. They can be bent, coiled, shaped, textured, and wrapped into alluring designs and patterns. This book will introduce you to making beautiful jewelry with wire and metal, using easy techniques that almost anyone can master. Whether you choose to try one of Anne Mitchell's variations on chain maille or Wendy Witchner's creatively curved wire designs, you'll find plenty of wonderful projects to get your creative juices flowing.

Wire and metal sheet come in various thicknesses called gauges. The higher the gauge number, the thinner the wire or sheet, so 24-gauge is thinner than 16-gauge, for example. Wire is available in many metals, including gold, fine silver, and base metals, but the projects in this book usually call for sterling silver wire. Sterling silver is an alloy that contains 92.5% pure silver. It is harder than fine silver (99.9% silver), but is still very easy to work with. Wire can be found at bead stores, jewelry-supply stores, mail-order and online merchants, and even some craft stores. Most stores carry a limited variety of wire, though, so if you're looking for something in particular, you may find you need to consult mail-order or online merchants.

Wire also comes in different hardnesses—dead soft and half-hard being the most commonly used. Unless otherwise noted, these projects should be made with half-hard wire.

Furthermore, wire is available in a wide range of profiles, or shapes, including half-round, square, rectangular, twisted, and even patterned or textured. Check the "Resources" section on page 56 to find sources for some of the more hard-to-find varieties.

If you're new to wirework, buy some inexpensive copper or craft wire in the gauge you want to work in and practice the techniques your project calls for. It's better to experiment with base metals

WIRE GAUGE CONVERSION CHART

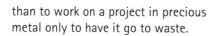

Gauge size	Diameter (inches)	Diameter (mm)	Profile
12	0.081	2.05	●
14	0.064	1.63	●
16	0.051	1.29	●
18	0.040	1.02	•
20	0.032	0.812	·
22	0.025	0.644	·
24	0.020	0.511	·

than to work on a project in precious metal only to have it go to waste.

SAFETY PRECAUTIONS

Be very careful when working with wire—especially when cutting it. Hold a finger over the part you're cutting off or slip the wirework into a plastic bag to prevent little pieces of wire from flying around. Wear eye protection. Always file the ends of your wire smooth or pinch it down with pliers to prevent it from catching on skin or clothing.

TOOLS

Just a few basic tools are required for making beautiful wire jewelry:
Chainnose pliers (a) have smooth, flat inner jaws, and the tips taper to a point so you can get into tiny spaces. Use them for gripping and for opening and closing loops and rings.

Flatnose pliers are similar to chainnose pliers, but the tips do not come to a point. They're useful for gripping and bending wire.

The curved tips on **bentnose pliers (b)** allow you to work at different angles than you would with chainnose pliers. When opening and closing jump rings, it's helpful to use at least one pair of bentnose pliers to avoid having your hands bump into each other.

Roundnose pliers (c) have smooth, conical, tapered jaws. You can form loops around them.

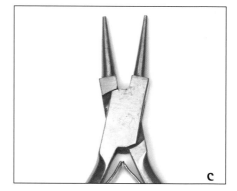
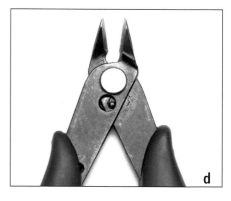

A small **ball peen hammer** is great for texturing and hardening metal and wire. For hardening without texture, use a **rubber mallet**.

On **diagonal wire cutters (d)**, the outside (back) of the blades meets squarely, yielding a relatively flat-cut surface. The inside of the blades makes a pointed cut. Always cut wire with the back of the blades against the section you want to use. **Flush** and **ultra-flush** cutters are similar to diagonal wire cutters, but they produce a smoother flat-cut surface.

LINKS AND WRAPS

LOOPS AND JUMP RINGS

Bending and wrapping wire are the core skills needed for making wire jewelry. Learn the techniques shown on this page and you'll be on your way to making the projects in this section, all of which are made with jump rings, wire links, or wrapped loops.

plain loops

1 Trim the wire ⅜ in. (1cm) above the top bead. Make a right-angle bend close to the bead.
2 Grab the wire's tip with roundnose pliers. Roll the wire to form a half circle. Release the wire.

3 Reposition the pliers in the loop and continue rolling.
4 The finished loop should form a circle centered above the bead.

wrapped loops

1 Make sure you have at least 1¼ in. (3.2cm) of wire above the bead. With the tip of your chainnose pliers, grasp the wire directly above the bead. Bend the wire (above the pliers) into a right angle.
2 Using roundnose pliers, position the jaws in the bend.

3 Bring the wire over the top jaw of the roundnose pliers.
4 Reposition the pliers' lower jaw snugly into the loop. Curve the wire downward around the bottom of the roundnose pliers. This is the first half of a wrapped loop.

5 Position the chainnose pliers' jaws across the loop.
6 Wrap the wire around the wire stem, covering the stem between the loop and the top of the bead. Trim the excess wire and press the cut end close to the wraps with chainnose pliers.

making jump rings

Jump rings can be made from any gauge wire, but thicker wire will produce a stronger jump ring. The dowel used determines the inside diameter of the links.
1 Drill a small hole through the dowel. The hole should be large enough to accommodate wire of your chosen gauge. Insert the end of the wire into the hole.

2 Wrap the wire around the dowel as many times as needed to make the number of jump

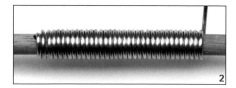

rings you want. Keep the wraps tight and close to the previous wrap.
3 With the wire cutter flush against the last wraps, cut the excess wire off both ends and and remove the coil from the dowel.

Do not use diagonal wire cutters to make jump rings; because one end is cut at an angle, the jump rings will not close properly. You may use double flush cutters, such as Ultraflush by Lindstrom, to cut the coil one loop at a time, down the length of the coil.

A faster and better way requires a benchpin and a jeweler's saw. Position the coil against a bench pin (see Sawing metal, p.48). Use a jeweler's saw with a size 5/0 blade and hold the saw frame in a vertical position so the blade will not stick or break. Gently pull the blade down the side of the first coil. As you cut one ring, the blade also cuts into the adjacent ring, putting you in position for the next cut. Repeat along the length of the coil.

opening and closing loops and jump rings

1 Hold the plain loop or jump ring with two pairs of chainnose pliers or chainnose and bentnose pliers.
2 To open the loop or jump ring, bring the tips of one pair of pliers toward you and push the tips of the other pair away from you.

3 String beads, chain, or other elements on the open loop or jump ring. Reverse the steps to close.

Wire link chain

Make a sturdy yet beautiful chain to highlight handblown art glass beads or polished stone nuggets, as shown here. To lend the silver an antique look, finish with a liver of sulfur bath and some gentle polishing.

DESIGN THE NECKLACE

The chain accounts for about 5 in. (13cm) of this 17-in. (43cm) necklace. Adjust the length of the bead strand to lengthen or shorten the overall length, if desired.

❶ Arrange 12 in. (30cm) of gemstones and/or other beads on your work surface. Cut a 17-in. (43cm) piece of flexible beading wire and string the beads to the center of it.

❷ String a crimp bead, a large-hole bead, and a soldered jump ring on one end of the wire. Go back through the beads just strung plus a few more, then crimp the crimp bead (**photo a** and "Crimping," p. 9).

❸ Repeat step 2 on the other end (**photo b**), leaving a bit of slack in the strand to allow the beads to drape well.

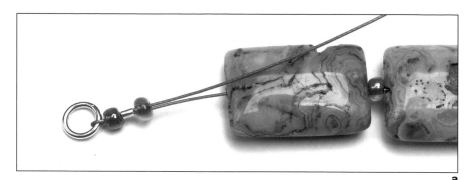

a

b

MAKE THE CHAIN

❶ Drill a hole approximately the same diameter as the 14-gauge sterling silver wire in the dowel and put the end of the wire in the hole.

❷ Wrap the wire around the dowel about 18 times. Be sure that each revolution is straight, tight, and flush against the previous wrap (**photo c**). Cut both ends with the flush cutter and remove the coil from the dowel.

❸ Pull the coils apart slightly to make room to insert the wire cutters. Skip one coil and clip the wire, using the cut end as a guide for the next cut (**photo d**). Always be sure that the flat cutting edge faces the component you're working on. Cut the angled end flush before cutting the next double coil. Repeat until you have eight double coils.

❹ Use flatnose pliers to bend and flatten each double coil into a figure 8 shape (**photo e**). Hammer the round ends several times to make the links stronger and more attractive.

❺ Smooth the hammer marks and any sharp edges with wet/dry sandpaper used wet. Start sanding with the coarser grit and end with the finer grit.

SHAPE THE HOOK-AND-EYE CLASP

❶ Make a ³⁄₁₆-in. (5mm) diameter wire loop using roundnose pliers (**photo f**).

❷ To make the hook, position the pliers about ¼ in. (6.4mm) below that

loop and make a partial loop in the opposite direction (**photo g**). Cut the wire just below the top of the first loop and shape the hook as shown in **photo h**.

❸ For the eye, make a loop as in step 1, above. Position the pliers as in step 2 and make a slightly larger loop (**photo i**). Hammer the hook-and-eye closure as in step 4 of "Make the chain."

❹ Sand the clasp as you did the chain in step 5 of "Make the chain."

FINISH THE CHAIN (OPTIONAL)

If you wish, apply a patina to the chain for an antiqued finish. Or, for a brighter look, skip ahead to the next section

❶ Prepare a small batch of liver of sulfur. (This is a strong chemical. Follow the directions on the bottle carefully.) Dip the chain into the liquid briefly until the silver becomes dark gray.

❷ Remove the chain from the liver of sulfur and rinse well under cool water. Dry the chain and rub it with extra-fine steel wool to remove any excess black.

❸ Polish the chain with a polishing cloth. When you're done, the sterling silver will have acquired a slightly antiqued finish.

c

d

ASSEMBLE THE NECKLACE

❶ Open one loop of a figure-8 link and attach it to the jump ring on one end of the bead strand. Attach a second link to the first and a third to the second. Repeat on the other side.

❷ Attach the clasp's hook portion to one end of the necklace and the eye to the other end.

❸ If you'd like the option of wearing your necklace at a longer length, make an expansion chain using additional figure-8 links.

e

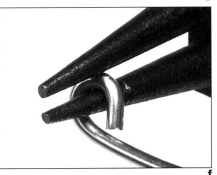

f

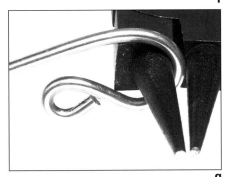

g

h

i

Designed by Vicky Jousan, who owns VJ of Scottsdale, a gallery featuring jewelry, paintings, and sculpture. Contact her at vicky@vjdesigns.com, or visit her website: www.vjdesigns.com.

MATERIALS

- polished stones and sterling silver beads to make a 12-in. (30cm) strand
- flexible beading wire, .024 for heavy beads, .019 for average or lightweight beads
- 23 in. (58cm) 14-gauge sterling silver wire
- 2 crimp beads
- 2 heavy-gauge sterling silver soldered jump rings

Tools: chainnose, crimping, flatnose, and roundnose pliers, flush or ultra-flush cutters, hammer, ¼ in. (6mm) dowel, 320- and 600-grit wet/dry sandpaper

Optional: extra-fine steel wool, polishing cloth, liver of sulfur

Crimping

While crimps can be flattened with chainnose pliers, crimping pliers provide a professional-looking finish. Crimping pliers have two grooves in their jaws to fold or roll a crimp into a compact shape.

To make a folded crimp:

1

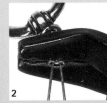

2

3

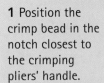

4

1 Position the crimp bead in the notch closest to the crimping pliers' handle.

2 Separate the wires and firmly squeeze the crimp.

3 Move the crimp into the notch at the pliers' tip and hold the crimp as shown. Squeeze the crimp bead, folding it in half at the indentation.

4 Test that the folded crimp is secure.

Caged beads

Make a lovely pendant and matching earrings by using this simple technique to wrap your favorite beads. Make sure to practice the technique with some inexpensive copper wire of the desired gauge before working with sterling silver or gold-filled wire.

NECKLACE

❶ Cut two 12-in. (30cm) pieces of wire. Twist them loosely together a few times about 5 in. (13cm) from the ends. Gently bend one wire at a right angle to the other. Hold the twist in your nondominant hand with the chainnose pliers. Using your dominant hand, wrap the bent wire around the other wire firmly for about ½ in. (1.3cm), keeping the coil tight (photo a).

❷ String the 12mm bead on the two 5-in. ends. Bend the wrapped section into a curve with roundnose pliers and put the shorter wire end through the bead's hole (photo b). Do not put the longest end through. Holding the bead in your left hand, pull all three wires through the bead. Snug up the wrapped loop against the bead's hole. Trim the three ends to ³/₁₆ in. (5mm). Treating the three ends as one, form a small loop with the roundnose pliers (photo c).

❸ With the remaining piece of wire, start wrapping around the base of the coiled loop. Keeping the wraps close, continue wrapping around and down the top of the bead three to seven times. Spiral the eighth wire wrap down to the bottom loop. Holding the bead firmly with the top loop pushed against it, wrap the bottom loop 2–3 times, wrapping toward the bead (photo d). Trim the wire as close as possible and push in the end with chainnose pliers.

❹ String the wrapped bead and half the clasp on the linen. Tie the clasp on with a multiple overhand sliding knot, as follows:

MATERIALS
- 12mm gemstone bead
- 2 7mm gemstone beads
- 6 ft. (1.8m) 24-gauge silver or gold wire, half-hard
- 1 yd. (.9m) 2.5mm waxed linen
- clasp
- 2 earring wires

Tools: chainnose and roundnose pliers, diagonal wire cutters

Place about 6 in. (15cm) of cord tail alongside the cord length. Then wrap the tail loosely around both strands, working down toward the loop. Keep the wraps uncrossed. After the last wrap, bring the tail up through the wraps (figure).
Tighten it carefully to keep them from crossing. Pull the cord length to tighten the loop. Repeat with the other half of the clasp (photo e).

EARRINGS

❶ Repeat steps 1–3 with a 7mm bead.
❷ Open the loop on an earring wire, attach the dangle, and close the loop.
❸ Make the second earring to match the first.

Designed by Linda Salow, who can be reached at 270 Big Horn Dr., Estes Park, Colorado 80517, (970) 577-0439, lsalow@peakpeak.com.

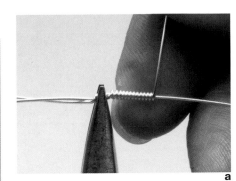
a

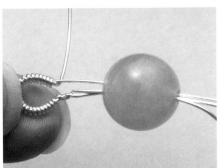
b

c

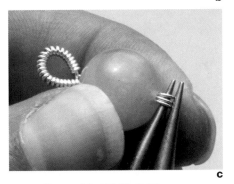
d

e

Wrapped hoops

Create your own hoop earrings with sterling wire, pearls, gemstones, and crystals.

CRYSTAL EARRINGS

❶ Cut a 7-in. (18cm) piece of 20-gauge wire. Wrap it snugly around a film canister or small bottle. Approximately 1½ in. (3.8cm) from one end, bend the wire upward (photo a). Remove from the canister.

❷ With roundnose pliers make a loop ¼ in. (6mm) above the circle. Bend the tail down so that it is flush with the stem and trim it where it meets the circle (photo b). File the end if necessary.

❸ Place the wire on the canister as before. Wrap the remaining tail around the stem from the bend to the loop (photo c). Trim the excess wire and remove the hoop from the canister or bottle.

❹ Cut a 4-in. (10cm) piece of 24-gauge wire. Wrap one end tightly around the hoop two or more times. Trim the short end (photo d).

❺ String assorted beads on the wire. To connect the wire, wrap it around the hoop as before and trim the excess wire (photo e).

❻ Repeat steps 4 and 5, attaching wires to the hoop and existing wires as desired (photo f).

❼ To make an earring wire, cut a 2-in. (5cm) piece of 20-gauge wire. Make a plain loop (see "Plain loops," p. 6) at one end. Using your fingers or roundnose pliers, bend a curve in the wire ¼ in. above the loop. Bend the wire outward, as shown (photo g), and trim the excess. File the end.

❽ Open the loop on the earring wire and attach the loop of the beaded hoop. Close the loop (photo h). Make a second earring the mirror image of the first.

PEARL EARRINGS

❶ To begin, follow steps 1–3 of the crystal earrings.

❷ Cut a 12-in. (30cm) piece of 24-gauge wire. Starting at the top of the hoop near the stem, wrap one end of the wire around the hoop tightly two or more times. Trim the excess wire.

❸ String a pearl and wrap the wire around the hoop two to three times

a

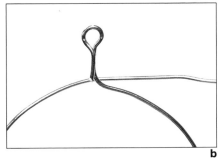

b

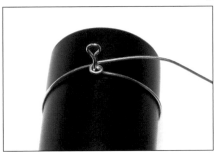

c

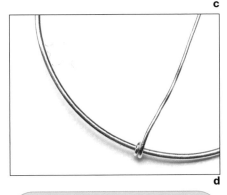

d

MATERIALS

- assorted crystals, pearls, or gemstones
- 18 in. (45.7cm) 20-gauge wire, half hard
- 8 in. (20cm) 24-gauge wire, dead soft

Tools: chainnose and roundnose pliers, diagonal wire cutters, metal file or emery board, film canister or small bottle

(photo i). Repeat until you reach the stem. Secure the wire with two or three more wraps and trim the excess.

❹ Complete the earrings as in steps 7–8.

Designed by Naomi Fujimoto. Contact her at nfujimoto@beadstylemag.com.

e

f

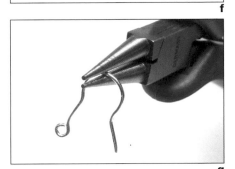

g

h

i

Angel pendant

Use an easy technique to wrap a shimmering abalone shell with wire. Add a few beads and make wire arms, wings, and a halo to complete this graceful angel pendant.

1 Measure the circumference of the abalone shell, add 4 in. (10cm), and cut five pieces of 22-gauge square wire to that length.

2 Hold one of the wires with your flatnose pliers and pull it through a polishing cloth to clean and straighten it. Repeat the process with the remaining four wires.

3 Working with one wire, center the shell on the wire and make four evenly spaced marks along the bottom of the shell where the four bindings will be (photo a).

4 Place the five wires side by side and bundle them together with a three-wrap bind at the marks using 22-gauge half-round wire (photo b).

5 Shape the bundled wires around the shell so the wire ends cross at the top (photo c). Remove the shell and place a three-wrap binding on each side just below the cross.

6 Use flatnose pliers to bend the wires up where they meet so they are parallel to each other (photo d). Check the fit again and make any adjustments necessary. Then bind all ten wires together above the bend (photo e).

7 Separate the wires above the bind into five pairs (photo f). String the pearl on one of the center wires and make a large wrapped loop (see "Wrapped loops," p. 6) above the pearl. Trim the excess wire.

8 Bring the remaining center wire up the back of the pearl and wrap it around the top of the pearl a few times to form the halo (photo g). Trim the

a

e

i

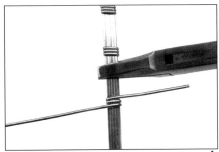
b

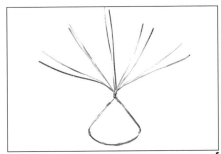
f

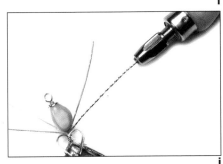
j

c

g

k

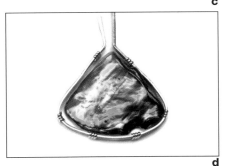
d

h

MATERIALS

- 1–1½ in. (2.5-3.8cm) abalone shell, triangular shape (Fire Mountain Gems, firemountaingems.com)
- 10–12mm pearl
- 4–6mm pearl
- 4mm bicone crystal
- 45 in. (1.1m) 22-gauge square wire, dead soft
- 10 in. (25cm) 22-gauge half-round wire, half hard
- snap bail

Tools: roundnose and flatnose pliers, wire cutters, fine-point marker or Sharpie, pin vise (available at some hardware stores, craft stores, and from online merchants), polishing cloth

excess wire and tuck the wire end in under the halo.

9 Set the shell in the wire frame. Use flatnose pliers to bend the edge wire on the front of the frame to hold the shell in place (**photo h**). Repeat on the back of the frame.

10 To form the arms and hands, bring the bottom two wire pairs down so they cross in a heart shape. End the wires decoratively with flat coils and loops (**photo i**).

11 Twist the remaining wires with a pin vise (**photo j**). Shape the wires to form the wings and attach the wires to

the back of the frame (**photo k**). Tuck in the wire ends.

12 Make a wrapped loop at the end of a 2 in. (5cm) piece of 22-gauge half-round wire. String the small pearl and a crystal and make a loop. Slide the wrapped loop onto one of the loops forming the angel's hands.

13 Attach the snap bail to the large wrapped loop above the halo.

Designed by Anna Lemons, whose work can be found at annalemonsjewelry.com. E-mail her at metroanna@aol.com.

Wrapped rings

Try this fun wire wrapping technique to make a chic ring. It's an easy way to showcase buttons and art beads and to accessorize your favorite outfits.

1 Determine the finished ring size.

2 Working two sizes larger than the finished size, hold a 24-in. (61cm) piece of wire against the mandrel. Position the wire with 10 in. (25cm) on the left of the mandrel and 14 in. (36cm) on the right.

3 Hold the wire in place with your nondominant hand and wrap the 14-in. length around the mandrel three times with your dominant hand.

4 Cross the wires on the front of the mandrel and adjust them, if necessary, so they are the same length.

5 Bend both wires perpendicular to the mandrel with chainnose pliers (**photo a**).

6 Slide the bead over both wires and against the mandrel (**photo b**). If you are using a button, position one wire in each buttonhole.

7 Hold the bead and the mandrel in your nondominant hand and hold the wires together just above the bead or button with your dominant hand. Twist the wires together by turning the mandrel and bead half way around.

8 Place your thumb on the hole of the bead and bend the wires against the bead (**photo c**). Gently apply pressure with your thumb to hold the wires snugly against the bead. Turn the bead and mandrel with your nondominant hand three or four times to form the wires into a coil at the center of the bead (**photo d**). Repeat until the coil is the desired size.

9 Bring the wires individually or together (depending on the shape of your bead) down the side of the bead

a

b

d

e

c

f

MATERIALS

one ring

- 1–3 12–20mm disk-shaped beads or buttons with 2mm holes (flower bead by Stephanie Sersich, www.sssbeads.com)
- 24 in. (61cm) 18-gauge wire, dead soft

Tools: roundnose and chainnose pliers, wire cutters, ring mandrel

and wrap them around the wires below the bead (**photo e**). Make two to three wraps.

⑩ Position the wires so they are on opposite sides of the bead above the band.

⑪ Remove the ring from the mandrel. Working one side at a time, wrap a wire around the band three to four times (**photo f**).

⑫ Use roundnose pliers to make a small coil with the end of the wire against the wraps if desired, or trim the wire on the inside of the band and squeeze it flush against the band with chainnose pliers.

⑬ Finish the remaining wire.

Designed by Jeannette Coons, owner of Girly Girl World. Reach her by mail at 19321 E. 40 Hwy., Studio D, Independence, Missouri 64055; by phone at (816) 795-9667; or by e-mail at girlygirlworld@sbcglobal.net. Visit her website, girlygirlworld.com.

Ancient rings

a

c

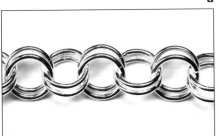

b

d

Known as ancient or Italian link, this design is a delicate-looking chain maille pattern. Though it appears complicated, it's actually a very easy technique to learn. You're sure to fall in love with the flowing links of this necklace and bracelet set. Use prefabricated jump rings or make your own, as shown on p. 6.

BRACELET

❶ Start with 30 closed jump rings and 28 open jump rings (see "Opening and closing jump rings," p. 6).

❷ Connect pairs of closed jump rings with pairs of open jump rings (**photo a**) until you have connected all 58 rings. This is a basic 2+2+2 chain (**photo b**).

❸ Repeat steps 1–2 to make a second chain.

❹ Open 30 jump rings.

❺ Starting at one end of the first chain, attach two jump rings to the first pair of rings. Skip the next pair of rings and add two jump rings, one on each side, to the third pair (**photo c**).

❻ Continue adding two jump rings, one on each side, to every other pair of rings on the chain.

❼ Repeat steps 4–6 with the second chain.

❽ Open a 4mm jump ring and attach a clasp loop to the end pair of rings on one chain between the two floating rings (**photo d**). Repeat with the second chain and the clasp's second loop. Connect the other end of the chains to the remaining clasp half.

NECKLACE

Follow the steps for the bracelet, with 68 closed jump rings and 64 open ones for each chain to make a necklace 17½ in. (44cm) long.

Designed by Anne Mitchell, who sells custom jump rings for this design. To order her jump rings, visit her website, annemitchell.net or e-mail her at anne@annemitchell.net.

WEIGHING SILVER

Troy weight is an ancient system of measuring precious metals and gemstones. It is derived from the troy system, which predates the eleventh century. The name comes from the city of Troyes in France, an important trading city in the Middle Ages. One troy oz. equals 31.10 grams. A standard ounce weighs 28.35 grams.

MATERIALS

both projects
- 4 4mm jump rings
- two-strand silver clasp (pacificsilverworks.com)

Tools: 2 pair chainnose pliers or **1** pair chainnose and **1** pair bentnose pliers

7¾-in. (20cm) bracelet
- 1.5 troy oz. (47g) sterling silver jump rings, 6.5mm inside diameter, 18-gauge wire (Anne Mitchell, style code SS)

17½-in. (44cm) necklace
- 3.5 or 4 troy oz. sterling silver jump rings, 6.5mm inside diameter, 18-gauge wire (Anne Mitchell, style code SS)

To make this anklet variation, make a single chain (steps 1–3 and 5–7) 9½ in. (24cm) long and attach a large lobster claw clasp with a 4mm jump ring. Add silver charms on the floating rings on one side of the chain for an anklet that dances around your leg with every step.

Scroll-link bracelet

People often ask how each link is made for this seemingly intricate project. It's up to you whether or not you want to tell them just a single pair of roundnose pliers did the job.

First, make the scroll links and jump rings. Then connect the links and attach the clasp.

MAKE THE LINKS

❶ This bracelet has eight scroll links per inch (2.5cm). Determine the finished length of the bracelet and subtract one inch (2.5cm) for the clasp. Multiply the result by eight and cut that number of 1½-in. (3.8cm) long pieces of wire. For a 7-in. (17.8cm) bracelet, cut 48 pieces. Cut 56 for an 8-in. (20cm) bracelet.

❷ Make sure the wire ends of each piece are cut flush and remove any burrs with a metal file.

❸ Turn a medium-sized loop at one end of a piece of wire (see steps 2 and 3 of "Plain loops," p. 6).

❹ Turn a second loop at the other end of the wire in the same direction. Both loops will be on the same side of the wire (**photo a**).

❺ Center the wire in the largest part of the pliers' jaws, with the loops curling up (**photo b**).

❻ Use your fingers to fold the wire around the bottom jaw of the pliers until the loops touch (**photo c**).

❼ Flatten the link by squeezing it with chainnose pliers.

❽ Repeat steps 3–7 with the remaining pieces of wire.

MAKE THE JUMP RINGS

Follow the directions on page 6 for making jump rings or use the following

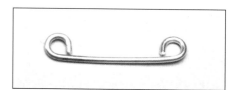

a

b

c

alternate instructions to make 80–90 jump rings.

❶ Bend the remaining length of wire in half.

❷ Place the dowel against the bend in the wire and hold it in position with your hand. With your other hand, wrap the wire in a coil around the dowel (**photo d**).

❸ When you reach the end of the first half of the wire, turn the dowel and wrap the other half.

❹ Slide the coil off the dowel and snip off the very end of the wire so it is flush. Place the cutters next to the flush end and cut the ring directly above (**photo e**), so both ends of the jump ring will be flush. Trim the angled end of the coil flush and continue cutting each ring in the same manner.

CONNECT THE LINKS

❶ Open four jump rings (see "Opening and closing loops and jump rings," p. 6).

❷ Stack four scroll links so the loops line up. Connect the links by sliding a jump ring through the loops on one end of the stacked links (**photo f**). Close the jump ring.

❸ Attach a second jump ring to the same loops.

❹ Repeat steps 2–3 with the other loop on the stacked links and separate the links into two stacks of two links (**photo g**).

❺ Repeat steps 1–4 with the remaining scroll links.

❻ Connect two links of one assembly with two links of a second assembly using three jump rings (**photo h**).

❼ Flip one side on top of the other so the jump ring trio is on the end.

❽ Connect two assemblies to the other end with three jump rings (**photo i**). Continue connecting the remaining assemblies, and end with three jump rings on each end.

ATTACH THE CLASP

❶ Connect three jump rings to the ring trio on each end of the bracelet.

❷ Open two jump rings and slide them onto an end jump ring trio. Attach the clasp to these two jump rings before closing them (**photo j**).

❸ Repeat step 2 on the other end of the bracelet and attach a single jump ring in place of the clasp.

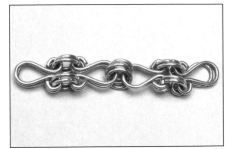
d

e

f

g

h

i

j

MATERIALS
- 12–14 ft. (3.7–4.3m) 18-gauge wire, sterling silver
- lobster claw clasp with loop

Tools: chainnose and roundnose pliers, flush or ultra-flush cutters, ³/₁₆-in. (5mm) wood dowel, metal file

Designed by Rachel Nelson-Smith of The Jewelry Workshop. Contact her by mail at PO Box 8331, Santa Cruz, California 95061; by phone at (408) 348-7003; or by e-mail at contact@msrachel.com. Visit her website, msrachel.com, to see more of her work.

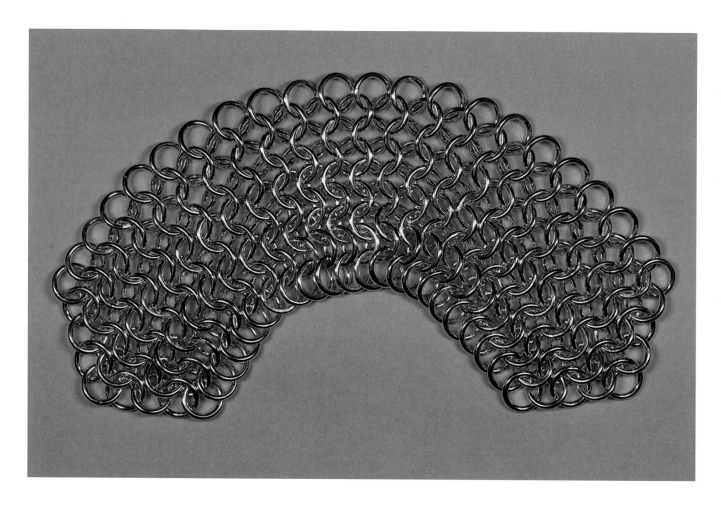

Flat mesh bracelet

Link jump rings together to make this strong, intriguing mesh bracelet. Use prefabricated jump rings or make your own (see "Making jump rings," p. 6).

PREPARE THE RINGS
Start with 110 closed and 88 open jump rings (see "Opening and closing loops and jump rings," p. 6). Try to make the seam on the closed rings as invisible as possible. These rings will form the body of a 7½-in. (19cm) bracelet.

ASSEMBLE THE RINGS
❶ Create a length of chain consisting of five sets of double rings connected by four single rings (photo a). The single rings are blackened in the photos.
❷ Lay out the length of chain as shown in photo a. Arrange the rings so the single rings are pointing up and

away and the sets of double rings are pointing down and towards the padded work surface, as shown in photo b. Secure the chain to the work surface with T pins to stabilize the chain and maintain the pattern as links are added. Working from left to right, number the lower row of rings 1 through 5.
❸ Put two closed rings onto a single open ring (photo c).
❹ Place the open ring under rings 1 and 2 of the lower row (photo d). The orientation of the two closed rings is important: the left side of the open ring needs to grab ring 1, and the right side of the open ring will grab ring 2. Close the jump ring.
❺ Place a single closed ring onto an open ring (photo e).
❻ The left side of the new open ring will come underneath the new lower

ring and underneath ring 2. The right side of the open ring will come underneath the single ring 3 (photo f). Close the jump rings.
❼ Repeat step 6, attaching the open ring to rings 3 and 4 (photo g).
❽ Repeat step 6, attaching the open ring to rings 4 and 5 (photo h).
❾ Repeat steps 3–8 until you have completed 22 rows of chain.

TAPERING THE ENDS
❶ The tapering process begins by repeating step 3, but instead of placing two closed rings on an open ring, place one and keep the closed ring to the right side of the open ring (photo i).
❷ Continue across as shown in photo j.
❸ Don't place any closed rings onto the open one being attached to rings 4 and 5 (photo k).

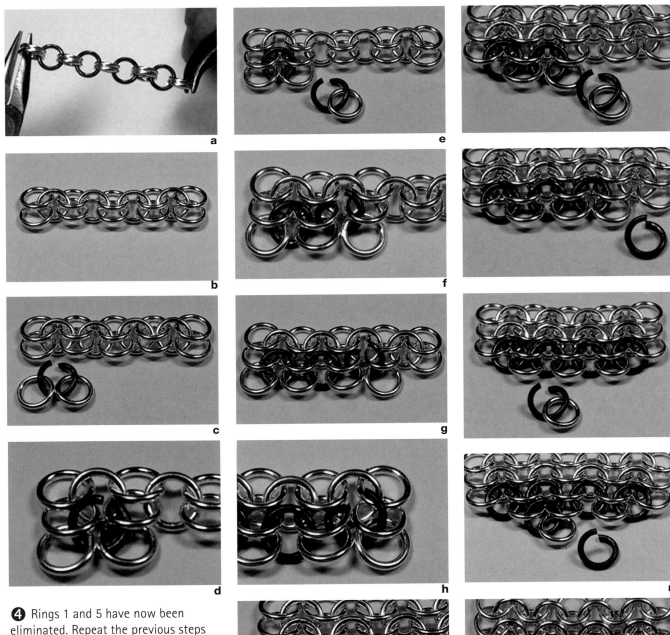

4 Rings 1 and 5 have now been eliminated. Repeat the previous steps to finish off the final row (**photos l, m, and n**).

5 Once one end of the tapering is complete, turn the bracelet over to work on the opposite end. If the bracelet is not turned over, the jump rings will be flipped in the wrong direction.

6 By now you should be a master at opening and closing jump rings. Use your perfected skills to attach a silver toggle or other clasp to the one remaining ring on each end.

Designed by Anne Mitchell, who sells custom jump rings for this design. To order her jump rings, visit her website, annemitchell.net, or e-mail her at anne@annemitchell.net.

MATERIALS
- 2 troy oz. (62g) 16-gauge sterling silver jump rings, 5.5mm inside diameter (Anne Mitchell, style code: RR)
- sterling silver toggle or other clasp

Tools: bentnose and chainnose pliers, padded work surface, T pins

Tryzantine
bracelet

a

d

g

b

e

h

c

f

i

This bracelet is a variation of the classic Byzantine link pattern. The density and weight of this chain make for a great bracelet or necklace. Admirers will wonder how you constructed such an intricate design.

In the process photos above, blackened jump rings are used to distinguish which rings to add in each step. As you work, watch the orientation of the paper clip as shown in the photos. Refer to page 6 for instructions on how to make your own jump rings, if desired, as well as how to open and close jump rings.

❶ Open three jump rings and connect them to three closed jump rings (photo a).

❷ Slide the outer two jump rings of one link section onto a paper clip (photo b).

❸ Connect two jump rings to the end three-ring link (photo c).

❹ Slide the left jump ring to the left so it rests against the jump rings on the paper clip. Repeat on the right with the right jump ring (photo d).

❺ Turn the assembly on its side (photo e).

❻ Open two jump rings and connect them to the center three rings (photo f).

❼ Place a closed ring between the two rings at the end of the chain. This ring is connected in the following step.

❽ Working with one jump ring at a time (photo g), connect three jump rings through the two end rings and the closed center ring just added (photo h).

❾ Connect two jump rings to the end three-ring link and slide them to the sides as before (photo i).

❿ Repeat steps 5–9 until the chain is the desired length.

⓫ Attach a lobster claw clasp to the end two-ring link with a jump ring. Connect a jump ring to the two-ring link at the other end of the chain.

Designed by Anne Mitchell, who sells custom jump rings for this design. To order her jump rings, visit her website, annemitchell.net, or e-mail her at anne@annemitchell.net.

MATERIALS

- 1.5 troy oz. sterling silver jump rings, 6.5mm inside diameter, 16-gauge wire (Anne Mitchell, style code TT)
- lobster claw clasp
- paper clip

Tools: 2 pair chainnose pliers or 1 pair chainnose and 1 pair bentnose

Wrapped loop necklace

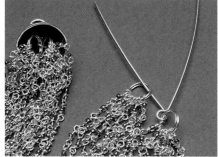

MATERIALS

- hank size 11º seed beads
- 2 wide bead caps (with 15mm openings)
- 56 yd. (51.2m) 24-gauge wire
- 8 in. (20cm) 20-gauge wire
- 4 7.5mm split rings
- clasp

Tools: roundnose and chainnose pliers, diagonal wire cutters

Composed of more than 1,000 wrapped loop units, this pretty necklace has a beautiful drape. While there's nothing difficult about the project, it is time-consuming because of the number of elements that need to be made.

❶ Cut 61 1½-in. (3.8cm) lengths of 24-gauge wire.

❷ Make a small wrapped loop on one end of one of the pieces (see "Wrapped loops," p. 6). String a seed bead and make a wrapped loop on the other end. Repeat for a total of 30 links.

❸ Begin a wrapped loop on one end of another piece of wire and pull it into the wrapped loop on a completed link (**photo a**). Complete the wraps. String a

bead and make the first half of a wrapped loop. Pull a finished link into the open loop (**photo b**) and complete the wraps. Continue connecting the links until the chain is 61 links long.

❹ Repeat steps 1–3 19 more times.

❺ Measure the length of each strand. Add or subtract links to even them out.

❻ String one end loop from 10 strands onto a split ring. Keeping the strands

in order, string the other end onto a second split ring. Repeat with two more split rings and the other 10 strands. Using a 4-in. (10cm) piece of 20-gauge wire, make the first half of a wrapped loop an inch (2.5cm) from one end of the wire. Pull two split rings into the loop (**photo c**) and finish the wraps.

❼ String a bead cap (**photo d**). Make the first half of a small wrapped loop on top of the bead cap. Add one half of the clasp and complete the wrap. Repeat steps 6 and 7 on the other end.

Designed by Linda Salow, who can be reached at 270 Big Horn Dr., Estes Park, Colorado 80517, (970) 577-0439, lsalow@peakpeak.com.

COILS AND SHAPES

WIRE SHAPES AND COILS

Once you've gotten accustomed to the basics of wirework, you can branch out and add new skills and techniques to your personal toolbox. Incorporating coiled and shaped wire elements in your jewelry is a great next step. Use coiled wire to accent a necklace, like the one shown on page 32, or on a ring band, as shown on page 34. Make shaped wire links for a raku necklace, like the one on page 40, or make curvy earrings like those on page 42. Whatever you choose, you're sure to find these techniques fun and inspiring.

Making wire coils

Coils are made by wrapping one piece of wire around another. The coiled piece is then removed from the core, cut to the desired length, and strung in place. Follow the instructions below to make your own coils.

1 Determine the length and gauge of wire you want to use for the coil and fold it in half (approximately 8-9 in. (20-23cm) of wire will make 1 in. (2.5cm) of coil). Also, determine what gauge you'll use for the core. Place a length of core wire inside the fold. Begin making the coil by wrapping one end of the wire around the core. Keep the wraps close together. When the first half is coiled, repeat with the other end of the wire.

2 Remove the coil from the core and cut pieces to the desired length. File the ends smooth before using.

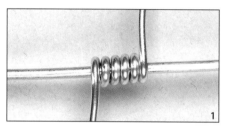

Shaping wire

Wire can be bent, curved, folded, and even tied in knots. There's almost no limit to the forms wire can take. For consistency and replicating shapes exactly, try using a wire jig. A jig is a board that has holes laid out in a grid pattern into which you place pegs of varying sizes. The placement of the pegs forms a pattern around which the wire is curved.

Wire can also be shaped freehand, with or without the assistance of tools. Take your time when shaping wire. The extra effort will pay off.

Texturing and twisting wire

Give your wire projects an artistic flair by texturing or twisting it. To give your wire texture, simply place it on a steel block or anvil and hammer it gently with a small hammer. Wire hardens as it is hammered, so be sure to do your texturing after it is already shaped as it will not bend easily once it's been hammered.

Using twisted wire is another way to impart visual interest to wire projects. It's easiest to purchase twisted wire but you can also make your own if desired. To make twisted wire, cut a piece of round wire that is two-and-a-half times as long as the desired length of twisted wire. Fold the wire in half and place the cut ends in a vise. Slide a pencil or other cylindrical object in the bend and, keeping tension on the wire, begin twirling the pencil around. The wire will begin to twist. Keep twirling the pencil until the wire has achieved an adequate twist. Cut both ends and file smooth.

Beaded wire earrings

Use custom-made wire coils as spacer beads, as shown in these fast and easy earrings. Try using wire coils in place of cylindrical spacers for other projects as well, varying the length of the coil, the gauge of the coil wire, or the diameter of the core around which you make the coils.

Once you begin, work slowly. Thin, 24-gauge wire bends easily so don't apply too much pressure to the dangles.

❶ Cut the wire into the following pieces: two 2¼-in. (5.7cm), two 1½-in. (3.8cm), two 1-in. (2.5cm), one 15-in. (38cm), and one 5-in. (12.7cm). Optional: to add a slight curve to the dangles, place each dangle on a large curved surface such as a drinking glass and gently bend the wire over it.

❷ With the very tips of the roundnose

pliers, make a small loop (see "Plain loops," p. 6) ⅛ in. (3mm) from one end of all the wires except the 15- and 5-in. pieces.

❸ Bend the 15-in piece in half. Place the 5-in wire in the bend (photo a). Hold the wires in your nondominant hand. In your dominant hand, with firm pressure, tightly wrap the 15-in. piece around the 5-in. piece, keeping the coils very close together (photo b). When you reach the end of the first half of the wire, turn it and wrap the other half. Be careful to not wrap too tightly, however, or you may find it difficult to remove the coil from the core. When the coil is about 3 in. (7.6cm) long, cut the ends off. Pull out the 5-in. piece. Cut the best sections of the coil into six pieces, each about ⅜ in. long. Trim the wire ends if they are sticking out.

❹ String three seed beads on each 2¼-in. piece of wire, two seed beads on each 1½-in. piece, and one seed bead on each 1-in. piece.

❺ String a coil on each of the dangles. Then string three beads on the 2-in. pieces, two beads on the 1½-in. pieces, and one bead on the 1-in. piece.

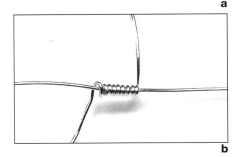

❻ Make a small loop on the end of each dangle.

❼ String five beads on a wire hoop earring. Then string a 2¼-in. dangle, a seed bead, a 1½-in. dangle, a seed bead, a 1-in. dangle, and five seed beads. Repeat for the other earring.

Designed by Sue Raasch, a nurse living in Missoula, Montana.

MATERIALS

- **48** size 11º seed beads
- **40 in. (1m)** 24-gauge sterling silver wire, half-hard
- **2** hoop earrings, 1-in. (2.5cm) diameter

Tools: roundnose and chainnose pliers, diagonal wire cutters

Twists and turns

If you've never worked with wire before, here's a beginner's project that's fun and easy. Don't be deterred by how handsome the necklace and bracelet are—they really can be done with just a few tools and supplies.

To get comfortable with wirework and to develop a feel for turning shapes with pliers, practice with copper wire, which is less expensive than sterling silver. Follow the clasp templates at right and make a few sample spirals and hooks. Once you're familiar with the basic techniques of wireworking, you'll be ready to make this necklace and bracelet as well as several variations of your own.

This necklace consists of twisted wire coils interspersed with Bali beads on 16-gauge wire. (Each inch (2.5cm) of coil requires approximately 8 in. (20cm) of twisted wire.) Two optional finishing steps follow the basic directions. First, you can tone down the brightness of the silver wire by darkening the coils with an oxidizing chemical. If you omit

figure 1

figure 2

this step, the sterling silver wire will tarnish over time anyway. Second, you can hammer the clasp to flatten and harden the wire. Since this necklace calls for 16-gauge wire, the additional stiffness is not required.

❶ Bend the twisted wire in half. You'll work with half the wire at a time, so coil one section and secure it with a twist tie to keep it out of your way.

❷ Place the 16-gauge wire against the fold in the twisted wire and hold it in place with your left hand. With your right hand, wrap the twisted wire around the 16-gauge wire as if you were making a tight spring (photo a). Keep the wraps close together.

❸ When you reach the end of the first section of twisted wire, turn the piece around and continue wrapping with the other half.

❹ Slide the completed coil off the wire core. With your wire cutters, cut the coil into eight 1-in. (2.5cm) segments and one 7-in. (18cm) segment (photo b). Avoid stretching or distorting the coil as you cut.

❺ Slide the 7-in. coil onto the center of the 16-gauge wire. This becomes the back of the necklace. String a symmetrical pattern of coils and Bali beads onto each end of the 16-gauge wire.

❻ With roundnose pliers, coil the end of the 16-gauge wire into a small spiral following the template in figure 1 (photo c, left).

❼ Slide the entire length of coils and beads against the spiral before you work on the other end. Rest the

necklace on a flat surface and bend the exposed 16-gauge wire upwards into a right angle close to the end coil. Check the bead placement and the fit before you cut the exposed wire to approximately ⅝ in. (1.6cm). Grab the tip of the wire with roundnose pliers and rotate it into a U-shaped hook as in figure 2 (photo c, right).

❽ File the wire ends until smooth. String the pendant onto the spiral so it hangs from the bottom coil. The hook should catch the upper coil (photo d).

❾ With your fingers, shape the necklace until it is round and feels comfortable around your neck.

OPTIONAL FINISHING TECHNIQUES

❶ To darken the coiled wire, use an oxidizing (tarnishing) agent such as Black Max or liver of sulfur before stringing. Follow the product directions, then polish the silver gently with a treated cloth to bring out the silver's highlights (photo e).

❷ Pad a solid work surface with leather and tape a piece of Ultrasuede or leather to the hammer's face before you begin to pound the wire. Work on the spiral before you finish the hook end so you can slide the coils away from the spiral when you pound. Pound both sides of the spiral until the wire is slightly flattened. Then make the clasp's hook end and repeat.

Designed by Wendy Witchner. Visit her website, wendywitchner-jewelry.com, to see more of her work.

MATERIALS

- 11 ft. (3.4m) 24-gauge twisted sterling silver wire (wire and tools available through Thunderbird Supply Co., 800-545-7968, thunderbirdsupply.com)
- 20 in. (51cm) 16-gauge sterling silver wire, dead soft
- 8 Bali silver beads or spacers (hole must fit over 16-gauge wire)
- pendant

Tools: chainnose and roundnose pliers, wire cutters, #2 metal file

optional supplies

- Black Max or liver of sulfur
- silver polishing cloth
- Ultrasuede or leather scraps
- hammer and steel block

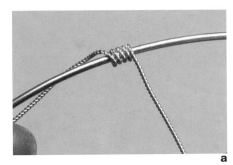
a

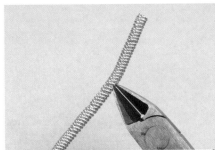
b

c

d

e

COILS AND SHAPES

Coiled collar

Large beads, such as the millifiori elbow bead used in this piece, can be challenging to use. Often they are too large and cumbersome for projects like bracelets, and they can overwhelm basic strung necklaces. Incorporating wire coils and shapes is the perfect solution. They provide substance and textural interest while focusing attention where it belongs.

MAKE THE COILS

When wire coils are a central part of your design, it is helpful to have several 15-in. (38cm) coils of various gauges on hand, so you can cut the size coil you need as you assemble the piece. Approximately 8–9 in. (20cm) of wire will make 1 in. (2.5cm) of coil.

❶ Determine the length and gauge of wire you want for the coil and fold it in half. (The coils shown here are made with 16-gauge wire.) Place a length of 14-gauge wire against the fold and hold it in place. With your dominant hand, wrap the coiling wire around the 14-gauge wire core (**photo a**).

❷ When you reach the end of the first half of wire, turn the piece and wrap the other half.

❸ Remove the coil from the 14-gauge core and cut the desired length (**photo b**). Clean up each end of the cut coil by cutting the wire end on a diagonal. Use a metal file to remove any burrs or rough edges.

❹ To make a flat coil, turn a small loop at the end of a length of wire. Continue turning the loop until it starts to wrap around itself (**photo c**).

❺ Grasp the loop with chainnose or flatnose pliers. Push the wire down and

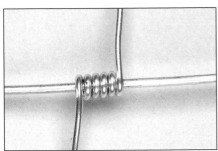

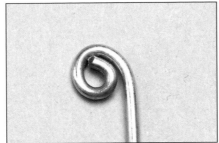

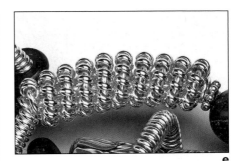

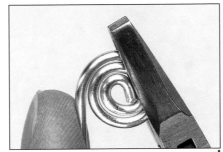

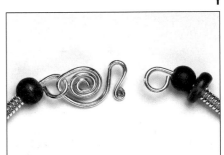

around the loop with your index finger (**photo d**). Reposition the coil in the pliers and continue to form the flat coil.

MAKE THE WIRE COMPONENTS

❶ String the focal bead on a 16-in. (41cm) length of 14-gauge wire.

❷ String a 16-gauge coil on each side of the focal bead. Because this focal bead is slightly off-center, I strung a ½-in. (1.3cm) coil on one side of the focal bead and a 1-in. coil on the other. To incorporate moving parts, string glass donuts with large holes over the coils. Then string a 5–8mm bead next to each coil.

❸ Center the beads on the 14-gauge wire. Finish each end with a flat coil. Make the center loop of the coil large enough to go over a 14-gauge wire and leave a small space after the beads for connecting the other wire components.

❹ Now make the remaining parts with 16-gauge wire. Cut several 6–14-in. (15–36cm) lengths and string each section with wire coils and beads. Arrange the sections as desired. To secure each section in place, wrap the wire tail two or three times around the focal bead component. Trim the excess wire or twist the ends into spirals or curls or whatever suits your design.

❺ To make a coiled bead (**photo e**), coil about 4 ft. (1.25m) of half-round 16-gauge wire around an 8-in.

16-gauge wire core. After coiling, center the coil on the wire core and spiral it around a pen or dowel.

❻ Pass one end of the core through the center of the flat coil on the focal bead component. Cut the wire end to about 2 in. beyond the flat coil. Grasp the end of the wire with roundnose pliers and curve it around the jaw to make a large loop. Repositioning the pliers as needed, continue rotating to make a triple stacked loop (**photo f**).

❼ String a few beads and a coil section on the other end of the core wire and then repeat step 6 to secure it in place.

MAKE THE NECK WIRE AND CLASP

❶ Cut a 7-in. (17.8cm) length of 14-gauge wire and make a large loop at one end. Attach the loop to the stacked loops on the end of the flat coil (**photo f**).

❷ String 5 in. (12.7cm) of 16-gauge coil and donuts or an accent bead. Make a large loop (see "Plain loops," p. 6) at the other end of the wire. Repeat to make the other side.

❸ Refer to the **template** at right to form the clasp with 14-gauge wire (**photo g**).

❹ Slide the clasp onto one of the loops made in step 2.

MATERIALS
- 2½-in. (6.4cm) focal bead
- 6 5–8mm beads
- 10 donuts with large holes
- assorted glass and metal beads
- 18 ft. (5.4m) 16-gauge wire
- 3 ft. (.9m) 14-gauge wire
- 2 ft. (61cm) 16-gauge half-round wire

Tools: chainnose or flatnose and roundnose pliers, diagonal wire cutters, metal file

Designed by Jude Carmona, a jewelry artist living in Steamboat Springs, Colorado. Contact her at judecarmona@aol.com.

Encrusted ring

The splash of color and sparkle of crystals dancing on your finger with every movement makes this ring an irresistibly perfect accessory.

1 String a 6mm crystal, a silver bead, and a 4mm crystal on a head pin and make a wrapped loop (see "Wrapped loops," p. 6). Make 20–22 similar dangles ½–⅝ in. (1.3–1.6cm) long.

2 Fold the 24-gauge twist wire in half and place the fold against the 18-gauge wire. Wrap one end of the twist wire in a tight coil around the 18-gauge wire (**photo a**). When you reach the end of the twist wire, turn it and repeat with the other end.

3 Slide the coil off the 18-gauge wire core and cut a 1½-in. (3.8cm) coil. Trim the ends of the coil on the diagonal so they are flush.

4 Repeat steps 2–3, coiling the round 24-gauge wire around the 20-gauge wire.

5 Center the round-wire coil on the 20-gauge wire and wrap it around the 18-gauge wire as in **photo a**. Slide the double coil off the wire.

6 Center the 1½-in. twist coil on the 18-gauge wire and shape it around a cylindrical object (**photo b**).

7 Place the ring on your finger with the coil centered at the base of your finger. Adjust the shape of the ring until it fits.

8 Cut two double coils five wraps long. Slide one coil on each end of the wire. Check the fit and adjust the length of the coils if necessary (trim them to

a

c

e

b

d

f

MATERIALS

- 4 in. (10cm) 18-gauge wire
- 4 in. 20-gauge wire
- 12 in. (31cm) 24-gauge wire
- 12 in. 24-gauge twist wire
- 22 1-in. (2.5cm) head pins
- 10–15 3-6mm silver beads
- 10–15 6mm crystals, bicone
- 15–20 4mm crystals, bicone

Tools: chainnose and roundnose pliers, diagonal wire cutters

shorten or stretch them slightly to lengthen) so there is about ½ in. of space separating the double coils on the top of your finger.

9 Make a hook on one end of the wire next to the double coil. With the other end of the wire, make a loop with about a 5/16 in. (8mm) diameter that is perpendicular to the hook (**photo c**). Don't trim the wire tail.

10 String half the dangles on the loop and against the double coil so they are on the back half of the loop. Catch the hook on the loop and squeeze it closed with chainnose pliers (**photo d**).

11 String the remaining dangles on the loop. Gently pull the wire tail with chainnose pliers until the dangles are snug. Wrap the wire around itself between the loop and the double coil (**photo e**). End the wrap on the top of the ring under the dangles.

12 Trim the excess wire and pinch the wire end down with chainnose pliers. **Photo f** shows the inside of the ring.

Designed by Wendy Witchner. Visit her website, wendywitchner-jewelry.com, to see more of her work.

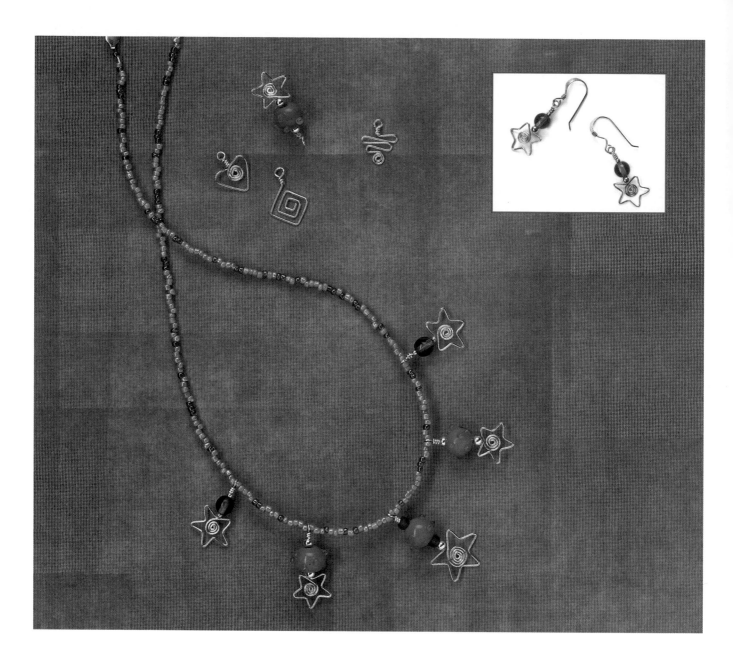

Fancy head pins

Create your first earring with a delicate star swinging from its end and you may never again be satisfied with a plain head pin. Fancy head pins look great with a bead strung onto them for an earring, perched on top of hair-sticks, or even as necklace or bracelet components, as shown above.

A good set of tools and lots of practice (start with 20-gauge copper wire) will help you get the hang of this project. Don't expect to make a perfect star the first or even the second time you try. But keep practicing.

After you've mastered stars, what other shapes can you imagine? Try forming the wire into hearts, diamonds, moons, or whatever you like.

Star head pins begin with a flat coil in the center. Then pull the wire into star points, forming it over the edge of chainnose pliers, as shown on p. 37.

MAKING FANCY HEAD PINS

❶ Cut a 6-in. (15cm) piece of wire. Grab the very end of the wire in the tip of your roundnose pliers and bend it around to make a tiny loop.

❷ Keeping the tip of the pliers in the center of the loop, roll it over onto itself one more time so it forms the beginning of a flat coil. Stop when the lower jaw of the pliers touches the wire length (**photo a**).

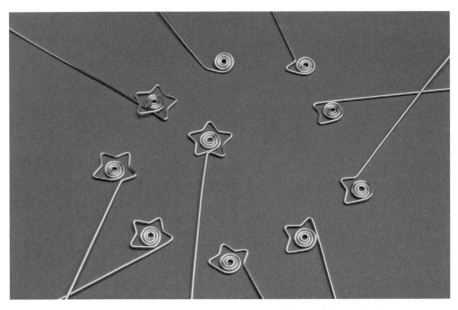

d

e

❸ Grasp the partially formed coil flat in the chainnose pliers (**photo b**). Hold it firmly but not so tightly that you mar the wire. Wrap the wire around the edge of the coil a quarter turn at a time. Reposition the pliers and repeat for about three revolutions.

❹ To form the first star point, grasp the wire at the base of the coil near the tip of the chainnose pliers. Hold the wire horizontally with the coil pointing up (**photo c**). Bend the wire over the edge of the top jaw of the pliers to meet the coil (**photo d**).

❺ Now visualize the shape of the star. (If this is difficult, draw a small star on paper and check your work against it after each bend to make sure the angle is correct.) Reposition your pliers on the second leg of the first point, and pull the wire down to form an angle of about 100–105 degrees to start the next point of the star (**photo e**).

❻ Reposition the pliers against the coil on the straight wire and pull the wire back over the top jaw to the coil (**photo f**), forming the second point. Continue bending points as described in steps 5 and 6 until you have completed the fifth point.

❼ Hold the wire as if starting a new point (**photo g**). Finish the head pin by bending it straight down between points 1 and 5.

❽ Repeat steps 1–7 to make as many head pins as desired.

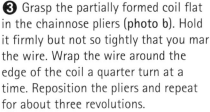

a

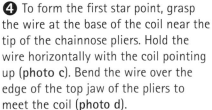

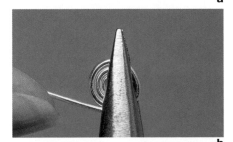

b

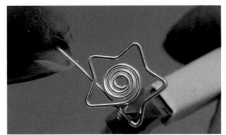

f

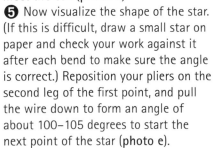

c

FINISHING THE COMPONENTS

String the desired beads on a fancy head pin and make a wrapped loop (see "Wrapped loops," p. 6) above the top bead. Make one or more additional components as needed to complete your project.

g

MATERIALS
- 20-gauge wire (half-hard sterling, brass, or other jewelry wire)
- assorted beads

Tools: roundnose and chainnose pliers, wire cutters

Designed by Mark Lareau, owner of The Bead Factory in Tacoma, Washington. He is the author of the book All Wired Up. *Check out the store website, thebeadfactory.com. Call (800) 500-BEAD for Mark's upcoming class schedule, or e-mail him at mark@thebeadfactory.com.*

opposite direction (**photo a, bottom left**). Trim the excess wire (**photo a, bottom right**). If the wire cutters leave chiseled points as shown in the photo, it's best to file the ends so the wire is flush against itself. This forms a more secure connection.

MAKING THE SPIRALS

❶ Bend a 9-in. wire in half and wrap it around the roundnose pliers to form a loop in the middle. Make a small loop on each end (**photo b**).

❷ Begin the spiral by rolling each end loop in on itself using chainnose pliers (**photo c**). If you put painter's (blue masking) tape on your pliers, you won't leave marks on the wire and you won't leave sticky residue on your pliers. Grip the loop in the pliers, push the length of the wire around it, and roll it into a flat spiral. Continuously reposition the pliers to keep the spiral flat and tight. Continue until there is about ¼ in. between the center loop and the spiral center. Repeat with the other half of the wire as shown in **photo d**.

❸ Place roundnose pliers between the center loop and the spiral. Bend the spiral down around the pliers (**photo e**). Repeat with the other side and adjust the spirals as needed (**photo f**).

❹ With one 7-in., one 5-in., and one 3-in. piece of wire from step 1, make three more spiral components, adjusting the number of turns for the shorter wires.

MAKING THE DANGLES.

❶ String a 3mm silver bead and a stone drop bead on a head pin and make a small loop at the top. If you are using a heavy bead, allow some extra wire for a wrapped loop (see "Wrapped loops," p. 6).

❷ Attach the dangle to the smallest spiral as shown in **photo g**. Optional: use a wrapped loop as in **photo h**.

PUTTING IT TOGETHER

❶ Open the loop of an S-link (see "Opening and closing loops and jump rings," p. 6) and slip it through the bottom of the center loop (where the wires cross) of the largest spiral, then close the loop.

❷ Open the other loop of the same

Spiral earrings

Wire coils and spirals have been used in jewelry throughout the ages, as is evident in Daniela Mascetti and Amanda Triossi's book, *Earrings: From Antiquity to the Present* (London, Thames & Hudson, 1999). These earrings feature overlapping spirals similar to those found in pre-Columbian jewelry. To make your own updated version, form the components, assemble the pieces, and adjust as needed.

GETTING STARTED

❶ Cut the wire into two 3-in. (7.6cm), two 5-in. (13cm), two 7-in. (18cm), and two 9-in. (23cm) pieces. Cut the remaining wire into six 1-in. (2.5cm) pieces.

❷ Make six S-links from the 1-in. wires. These connect the spirals, so the loops should be a uniform ¼ in. (6mm) each. Make a loop at one end using roundnose pliers (**photo a, top**). Make a loop at the other end facing the

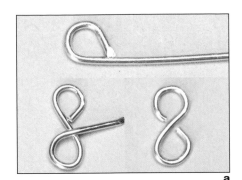

a

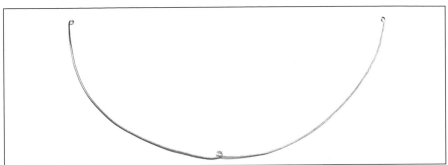

b

MATERIALS

- 5½ ft. (1.45m) 22-gauge wire, dead soft
- 4 in. (10cm) 22-gauge wire, half-hard, or 2 earring findings with loop
- 2 ½-in. (1.3cm) stone or glass drops
- 2 3mm silver or small daisy spacers
- 2 head pins

Tools: roundnose and chainnose pliers, wire cutters, ruler, needle file or sandpaper

c

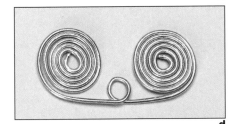

d

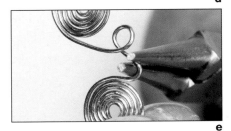

e

f

g

h

i

S-link and slip it through the top of the center loop of the next size spiral, and close. The largest spirals should overlap the next set and so on down the line.

❸ Connect the remaining spirals, including the smallest component with the dangle, the same way.

❹ Use your fingers and chainnose pliers to adjust the spirals as desired.

❺ Make a second earring to match the first.

EARWIRES

Open the loop on an earwire and attach it to the loop of the top spiral component. Close the loop. If desired, make your own earwires as follows:

❶ Cut a 2-in. (5cm) length of 22-gauge, half-hard wire (half-hard wire is best for findings as it holds its shape better, but if you use half-hard wire for the spirals, they won't be as easy to shape) and make a plain loop (**photo i, left**) or over-rolled loop (**photo i, center**).

❷ Bend the wire up as if you were going to coil it around the loop, but instead bend it in the other direction with roundnose pliers (**photo i, right**).

❸ Put a slight curve at the end of the earwire and trim to the desired length.

❹ Smooth the end with a needle file. If you don't have a file, rub the end of the wire on a piece of fine-grit sandpaper. Rinse the wire with a little rubbing alcohol or soapy water to get rid of any sandpaper residue before you wear the earrings.

Designed by Kelli Peduzzi, a freelance writer/editor and the author of several books. Visit her website, pureblissjewelry.com or e-mail her at kelli@pureblissjewelry.com.

COILS AND SHAPES

Shaped links

Link a diverse mix of beads with shaped wire links to make a stunning necklace. Make it even more interesting by incorporating a large centerpiece bead with extra holes in it. Stitch through the bead holes, using a length of wire as both a connector and an unexpected design element.

❶ Using 16-gauge wire, make the decorative connectors shown in the templates in **figure 1**. This necklace uses two As, two Bs, one C, and one D. (You can vary the combinations as you'd like, but you'll need at least one with a long tail as shown in D.) Bend the wire using your fingers and pliers.

❷ Hammer one or both sides of the connectors (**photo a**).

❸ Cut a length of 18-gauge wire for each bead that is ³/₄ in. (19mm) longer than the bead. String each bead onto its wire and turn a plain loop on each end (see "Plain loops," p. 6 and **photo b**).

❹ Working with your centerpiece bead, design a path for the wire. Cut a piece of 16-gauge wire slightly longer than you think you'll need. Make a large, open coil at one end (**photo c**).

❺ Working from front to back, go through any hole except those at the ends of the bead. Run the wire loosely across the back of the bead and come to the front through a neighboring hole. Continue sewing, and make your last pass through a hole at the edge. Use the tail to make a loop as shown in **photo d**.

❻ Working with connector D, curve the straight tail slightly and go through the available hole at the other edge. Keep the hammered side of the connector facing front. Bend the wire gently into a loop (**photo e**).

❼ Link connectors and beads to build

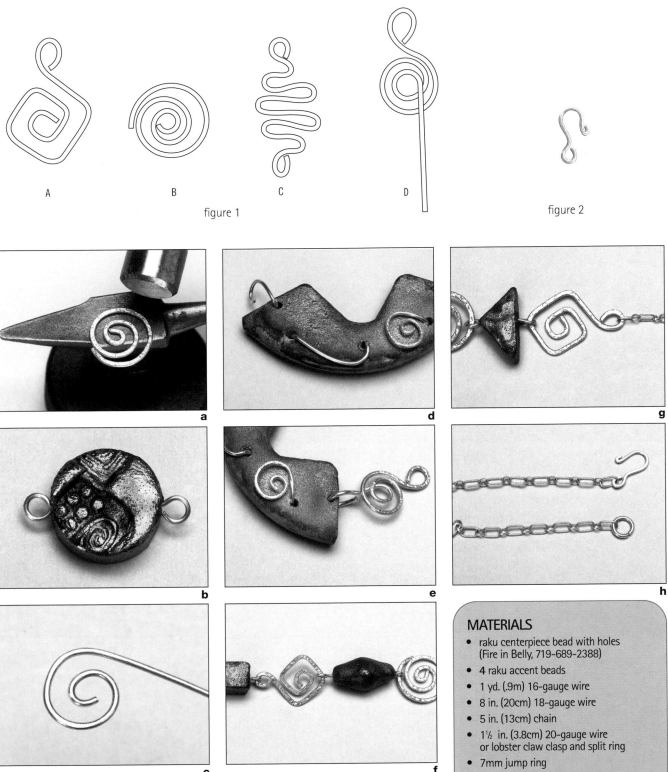

A

B

C

D

figure 1

figure 2

a

b

c

d

e

f

g

h

MATERIALS
- raku centerpiece bead with holes (Fire in Belly, 719-689-2388)
- 4 raku accent beads
- 1 yd. (.9m) 16-gauge wire
- 8 in. (20cm) 18-gauge wire
- 5 in. (13cm) chain
- 1½ in. (3.8cm) 20-gauge wire or lobster claw clasp and split ring
- 7mm jump ring

Tools: chainnose and roundnose pliers, wire cutters, ball peen hammer, and anvil or bench block

Designed by Wendy Witchner. Visit her website, wendywitchner-jewelry.com, to see more of her work.

the sides of the necklace (**photo f**).
❽ Cut the chain in half. Slide one end link into the loop on the last connector (**photo g**). Repeat on the other end of the necklace with the other piece of chain.

❾ Use 20-gauge wire to make a hook clasp (**figure 2**), hammer it slightly, and attach it to one end link. (Or attach a lobster claw using a split ring.) To finish the other end of the necklace, open a jump ring (see "Opening and closing loops and jump rings," p. 6) and attach it to the end link of the other piece of chain. Close the jump ring (**photo h**).

Sleek curves

Pearls and crystals adorn these delightful earrings. Because you wrap wire in tight spaces, these earrings take a little practice and dexterity.

❶ Cut a 6-in. (15cm) length of 14- or 16-gauge wire. Flush-cut both ends.

❷ Start at the top of the actual-size template (**figure**) and form a twice-around, slightly open spiral.

❸ Bring the wire out horizontally from the bottom of the spiral so it extends the width of the bead you wish to set in the first loop plus ⅛ in. or so (3-4mm).

❹ Curve the wire around a pen or wooden dowel with a diameter slightly greater than that of the bead (**photo a**).

❺ Make a second bend, as shown on the template, to fit the second bead.

❻ Bend the wire back just past the center and make a small bend.

❼ Make a final curve and end with a centered loop. Adjust the curves as desired, ensuring that the beads will fit in the appropriate curves. If desired, hammer it on both sides.

❽ Wrap a 3-in. (7.6cm) piece of 24-gauge wire around the top horizontal section of the wire two or three times, pressing the wraps together with chainnose pliers (**photo b**). String a pearl on the wire so it sits in the curve; adjust the wraps to position the pearl correctly if needed. Wind the wire around the bottom of the curve two or three times (**photo c**) and trim the excess.

❾ Attach a crystal between the outer edge of the spiral and the top of the bend on the other side as you did the pearl. Then attach a second large pearl in the large curve on the other side of the earring.

❿ Attach a crystal between the right and left curves. Then attach the third crystal below the second pearl.

⓫ String the third large pearl on a head pin and begin a ⅜-in. (1cm) wrapped loop (see "Wrapped loops," p. 6). Attach it to the loop at the bottom of the earring before finishing the wraps.

⓬ Open the loop on the earring wire and attach it to the top of the spiral. Close the loop.

⓭ Make the second earring the mirror image of the first.

MATERIALS

- 12 in. (30cm) 14- or 16-gauge wire, dead soft
- 3 ft. (.9m) 24-gauge wire, dead soft
- 6 7-8mm pearls
- 6 4mm bicone crystals
- 2 1½ in. (3.8cm) 24-gauge head pins
- 2 earring findings with loop

Tools: roundnose and chainnose pliers, diagonal wire cutters

Optional: hammer and anvil

a

b

c

Designed by Alice Korach, founding editor of Bead&Button *magazine. Visit her website, lostwaxglass.com, to see more of her work.*

Wraps with a twist

These whimsical pendants showcase raku donuts wrapped with twisted wire and accented with silver Bali beads and pearls. The three pendant styles described are just a starting point. Develop your own designs to suit the unique features of your components. You never know where a little experimenting might lead.

The raku donuts featured in the pendants above are made by Rory Raku (832-687-8361).

DONUT WITH ROUND PEARL DANGLE (ABOVE RIGHT)

❶ With the widest part of a pair of roundnose pliers, grasp the center of the 24-in. (61cm) length of twisted wire. Bend one side around one jaw of the pliers until it is parallel with the other side of the wire.

❷ Pass the bend through the center hole of the donut from back to front at an angle, so the bend is about ¼ –½ in. (6–13mm) above the top of the donut.

❸ Hold the wire in place with your nondominant hand; with your dominant hand, bend one of the tails up against the back of the donut so it is parallel to the wire on the front (photo a, p. 44).

❹ Pass the wire through the bend and wrap the wire tail back and under itself above the donut (photo b, p. 44). Make two more wraps around the wire bend below the first wrap. Use chainnose pliers to tighten each wrap before you start the next one (photo c, p. 44).

❺ Make sure the wire is pointing toward the front of the donut after the last wrap. Bend the wire over itself as if you were going to make another wrap, but pass it under both wires directly above the donut hole instead (photo d, p. 44).

❻ Repeat steps 3-5 with the other half of the wire.

❼ Curve both wires down toward the bottom of the donut until they cross.

❽ Grasp the wire on the left just above the cross with the tip of the roundnose pliers. Make a loop by

MATERIALS

donut with round pearl dangle (p. 43, right)
- 1½-in. (3.8cm) donut
- 24 in. (61cm) 20-gauge twisted wire
- 6-8mm sterling silver bead
- sterling silver bead cap
- 3mm sterling silver bead
- 6-8mm round pearl
- head pin

triangular donut (p. 43 center)
- 1½-in. (3.8cm) triangular donut
- ½-in. (1.3cm) donut
- 30 in. (76cm) 22-gauge twisted wire
- 2 6-8mm sterling silver beads

zigzag wrapped donut (p. 43, left)
- 1½-in. (3.8cm) donut
- 1 yd. (9m) 22-gauge twisted wire
- 3 in. (7.6cm) 22-gauge round wire, half-hard
- 2 6-8mm sterling silver bead
- stick pearl, vertical hole

Tools: chainnose, roundnose, and flatnose pliers, diagonal wire cutters, hammer, and anvil or block

figure 1   figure 2

wrapping the wire around one jaw of the pliers (**photo e**), repositioning the pliers, and continuing the loop so the wire crosses over itself and is pointing toward the bottom of the donut.

9 Use roundnose pliers to make an open coil similar to the template in **figure 1**. The open coil will be just below the bottom of the donut. Trim the excess wire.

10 Repeat steps 8–9 with the other wire but refer to the template in **figure 2** to form the open coil. The bottom of this coil is about ¼ in. below the first coil. Trim the excess wire.

11 Bring the left wire over the top of the right wire so the coils overlap.

12 Place the wire coils on an anvil or block. Use a hammer to flatten the wire slightly (**photo f**). Hammering will stiffen the wire and keep it in place. You can also lightly hammer the loops above the coils on the donut. Be careful to avoid cracking or breaking the donut.

13 Make a wrapped loop (see "Wrapped loops," p. 6) at one end of a 4-in. (10cm) piece of leftover wire. The loop should be large enough for your chain to pass through.

14 String a silver bead and make the first half of a wrapped loop in the same plane as the first. Slide the wire bend at the top of the donut (**photo g**) into the loop. Finish the wraps and trim the excess wire.

15 String a round pearl, a bead cap, and a 3mm round silver bead on a head pin. Make a loop (see "Plain loops," p. 6) close to the 3mm bead. Open the loop (see "Opening and closing loops and jump rings," p.6) and slide the loop on the bottom coil below the donut. Close the loop and string the pendant on a neck chain.

TRIANGULAR DONUT (P. 43, CENTER)

1 Cut a 22-in. (56cm) length of 22-gauge twisted wire and, using a triangular donut, follow steps 1–4 for the previous donut.

2 After the third wrap, bring one of the wires down behind the donut and through the center hole (**photo h**).

3 Wrap the wire around the side of the triangle and back through the center hole (**photo i**). Don't make the wraps too tight—you will tighten them in step 5. Repeat 6 times.

4 Repeat steps 2–3 with the other wire.

5 Make zigzags in the wraps to tighten them. Grasp the center of a wire wrap with the tip of the flatnose pliers and make a bend in the wire by turning the pliers about 30 degrees to one side (**photo j**). Repeat with all the wraps.

6 Trim both the wires near the bottom front of the donut. With the flatnose pliers, bend the wires in and down so the ends point down and lie against the donut.

7 Cut a 3-in. (7.6cm) length of 22-gauge twist wire. Bring ¾ in. (2cm) of one end through the hole of the ½-in. donut and bend it up against the back of the donut. Wrap the short wire around the long wire. Use chainnose pliers to tighten the wrap. Trim the short wire (**photo k**).

8 String a silver bead and make the first half of a wrapped loop. Slide the loop through the bend at the top of the triangular donut (**photo l**). Finish the wraps and trim the excess wire.

9 Repeat step 7 at the top of the ½-in. donut. String a silver bead and make a wrapped loop large enough to slide on a neck chain.

ZIGZAG WRAPPED DONUT (P. 43, LEFT)

1 Hold the roundnose pliers in your nondominant hand and grasp the center of a 1-yd. (.9m) length of 22-gauge twist wire in the jaws of the pliers. Bend the wire in a U shape around one jaw of the pliers and twist the wires together with your dominant hand (**photo m**).

2 Separate the wires in opposite directions above the twist so they are perpendicular to the loop. Place the donut between both wires against the twist (**photo n**).

3 Wrap one wire loosely through the hole until you've gone halfway around the donut (**photo o**). Repeat with the other half of the wire.

4 Wrap one wire around the other a few times (**photo p**) and trim the short wire. String a silver bead and make a wrapped loop large enough to slide on a neck chain.

5 Using the flatnose pliers, bend two zigzags in each wire wrap on both sides of the donut (see step 5, "Triangular donut").

6 String a stick pearl to the center of the 3-in. (7.6cm) round wire. Fold the wires up along the sides of the pearl. Cross them above the pearl and twist them together with your hand. String a silver bead over both wires and make a loop with both wires as one. Trim the excess wire, open the loop, and attach it to the bottom loop of the donut. Close the loop.

Designed by Wendy Witchner. Visit her website, wendywitchner-jewelry.com, to see more of her work.

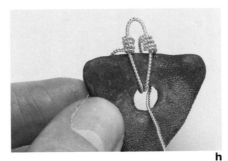

h

i

j

k

o

p

Daisy dangles

An all-occasion pair of earrings starts with these easy wire loops. Make daisy-shaped findings and hang a trio of crystal dangles. In a flash, you'll have something wonderful to wear.

❶ Cut an 8-in. (20cm) piece of 22-gauge wire.

❷ Grip the wire 1 in. (2.5cm) from the end with the larger part of the roundnose pliers. Wrap the long end of the wire around one jaw of the pliers. Reposition the pliers and continue wrapping the wire until it forms a loop (**photo a**).

❸ Hold the long end of the wire next to the loop and form a second loop the same size as the first (**photo b**).

❹ Make five more loops (**photo c**).

❺ Bring the first and last loops side by side and wrap the short wire end around the long wire a few times (**photo d**). Trim the excess wire as close to the long wire as possible.

❻ Place the wire finding on an anvil or steel block and flatten it slightly with a hammer to stiffen it.

❼ String a 4mm crystal and a round 2mm bead on the wire and against the wrap. Then make a plain loop (see "Plain loops," p. 6) above the beads (**photo e**).

❽ To make the center dangle, cut a 1½-in. (3.8cm) piece of wire and make a plain loop at one end. String a 2mm bead, 6mm bead, 2mm bead, crystal, and 2mm bead. Make a loop at the other end in the same plane as the first loop (**photo f**).

❾ Open the loop (see "Opening and closing loops and jump rings," p. 6) closest to the 6mm bead and slide a charm into the loop. Close the loop.

❿ Connect the top loop of the dangle to the center loop on the wire finding.

⓫ Cut a 1½-in. piece of wire. Trim the end of the wire so it is straight, as shown in **photo g, left**.

⓬ Place the end of the wire on an anvil or steel block and hammer the end until it is large enough to keep a 2mm

MATERIALS

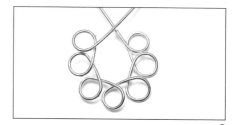

- 12 4mm bicone crystals
- 20 2mm round spacers
- 2 6mm beads
- 2 charms
- 25 in. (64cm) 22-gauge wire
- 2 earring wires

Tools: roundnose and chainnose pliers, diagonal wire cutters, metal file, hammer, anvil or steel block

bead from sliding off (**photo g, right**). Use a metal file to round the edges and remove any sharp points.

⓭ String a 2mm bead, crystal, 2mm bead, crystal, and 2mm bead on the wire. Make a plain loop above the beads (**photo h**).

⓮ Connect the dangle to the finding's third loop.

⓯ Repeat steps 11–13 to make another dangle and attach it to the fifth loop on the wire shape.

⓰ Attach the earring wire to the loop of the earring wire.

⓱ Make a second earring to match the first.

Designed by Wendy Witchner. Visit her website, wendywitchner-jewelry.com, to see more of her work.

c

d

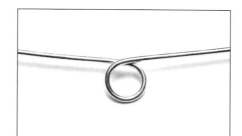

a

b

e

f

g

h

METAL

WORKING WITH METAL

Metal has been an essential material for jewelry makers for centuries. Although it is hard, metal is also malleable and can be easily worked and manipulated. It can be cut, bent, hammered, and shaped into nearly any form. Indeed, the appeal of metal may be as much its potential as its intrinsic value.

The following chapter is intended as a basic introduction to working with sheet metal. Techniques covered include sawing, piercing, riveting, and finishing. All connections for the following projects are cold connections—that is, they are made without the use of heat. Introducing heat to the metal-working process greatly expands the possibilities, but it also increases the safety issues and the need for additional equipment and chemicals. If you've never worked with metal or are hesitant about soldering, these are good projects for you to try.

METAL BASICS

Nowadays, most jewelers begin with metal that comes in sheet form. These sheets are measured in gauges like wire, so 20-gauge is thicker than 24-gauge, for instance.

A metal sheet is mounted on a bench pin and cut with a jeweler's saw loaded on a saw frame. Blades come in a variety of styles, from coarse to fine. Generally, you should match your saw blades to your metal sheet, so, if you're sawing a thin piece of metal, you should use a blade with relatively fine teeth. The blades are thin and not very flexible, so you'll break some blades before you get the hang of it. Coat the sides of the blade (not the teeth) with beeswax for lubrication. Reapply when the saw begins to sound scratchy. Practice on scrap metal, sawing along lines to build accuracy.

Follow these instructions to load the blade in the saw frame:
(a) Loosen the two blade screws.
(b) Make sure the teeth of the blade are angled down (away from the back of the saw frame).

a

b

(c) Slide the top of the blade between the saw frame and the top blade screw lug (farthest from the handle). Tighten.
(d) Insert the blade through a hole in the metal with the template facing away from the handle. Slide the metal to the top of the frame and let it rest against the frame, not the blade.
(e) Repeat step c with the bottom

screw, pushing the end of the saw frame against your work bench so the blade will be taut (photo a). Then tighten the screw.

SAWING METAL

Lay the metal flat on a bench pin, making sure you have enough room to saw and to maneuver the handle and the piece. Start the cut with an even, upward stroke to create a groove in which you can rest the saw blade. The actual cutting occurs when the blade is being pulled down. Gently push into the metal with the blade as you move the frame up and down with medium, even strokes. Always keep the blade at a 90-degree angle to the metal (photo b); it will break if not completely vertical or if you push too hard. The blade should practically carry itself forward into the metal as you saw up and down. To turn a corner or change the sawing direction, make faster, shorter strokes as you rotate the metal with your free hand. The saw should always stay in the same position. With practice, it will become second nature.

Copper corsage

Although it looks complex, you can make this pretty pin. You do not need a jeweler's torch or expensive buffers and sanders to make quality metal components. The basic metal-working tools are affordable (less than $100), and you can build on them, should you decide to continue with metals. You can also use them in other media. Either way, be creative, push yourself, don't be afraid to improvise with materials and tools, and most importantly, have fun.

The major steps in making the brooch shown here are cutting out the copper brooch; filing, shaping, and smoothing it; riveting the silver disk to the brooch center; making the silver stick pin; finishing the surfaces; and, finally, decorating the pieces with beads. It's important to practice using each of the tools (drill, saw, file, etc.) on scrap metal.

CUTTING OUT THE COPPER BROOCH

❶ Make a photocopy of **templates A** and **B** (p. 50) and cut them out in a square. Spread rubber cement on the back of **template A** (**photo a**) and affix it to the metal, making sure it's centered. Wait a few minutes for the glue to dry.

❷ Before you can cut out the design, you need to drill four holes (marked on the template) with a #52 drill bit. Work on a hard surface, preferably a wood

a

b

c

d

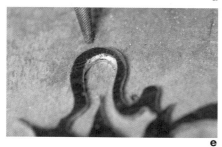

e

f

g

h

i

j

template A

template B

block, and mark the drill points with the center punch or nail by lightly striking the tool with a non-metal hammer (never strike a metal tool with a metal hammer) (**photo b**). Drilling these small indentations will help keep your drill bit from jumping and scratching the metal. Unless you have a drill press, drilling is tricky, so practice first. The holes allow you to slide the saw blade into the internal spaces of the design that must be removed. Creating these open internal areas is called piercing.

❸ Clamp the wooden bench pin to your work bench. The V-shaped notch in this essential tool allows you to support the edges of the metal while sawing. Lay the piece flat on the bench pin and trace the inside line of the design as you saw, maneuvering and turning the piece as you go. It may be easier to cut out several small sections instead of one large section. After removing the metal in the first opening in the design, loosen the bottom blade screw and remove the blade from the hole in the metal from this end. Insert the blade through the next hole, tighten it again, and cut out the next section.

❹ When you've sawn out all four openings, you can saw around the perimeter of the design. Be sure the bench pin supports the thin, ribbon-like portions of the piece. Otherwise, these areas will bend (**photo c**). When you've completed the sawing, peel off all the paper and any remaining glue.

FILING, SHAPING, AND SMOOTHING

❶ Gently file the sides of the ribbon with the file perpendicular to the metal. Keep filing until all the sharp edges have been removed (**photo d**).

❷ Use the half-round file to bevel the edges of the ribbon (**photo e**). This adds depth and gives the illusion of a ribbon with movement, rather than a strip of flat metal.

❸ Filing creates deep scratches that you remove by sanding with the different grits of sandpaper, starting with 220 grit and ending with 600 grit. The care you take in sanding determines the quality of your finished piece. Sand both the edges and the front surface. Sand in only one direction with a grit (**photo f**), but change direction when you change grits, sanding at a 90-degree angle to the previous direction. This enables you to see any deep scratches the previous grit did not remove.

RIVETING THE SILVER DISK

❶ Attach **template B** (the flower center) to the silver disk with rubber cement. Mark ten drill points with the center punch, remove the template, then drill ten holes with the #55 drill bit. (Note: only five holes are shown on the template as examples; add five more as you like.) File the front and back of the disk to remove burrs from the drill holes. Sand carefully (**photo g**).

❷ Now you need to drill holes in the copper piece for the first two rivets so the disk does not slip while you install the rest. Position the disk in the center of the copper piece. Go through two drilled holes on opposite sides of the disk with a Sharpie to mark the copper. Set the disk aside and drill the two holes in the copper with a #55 bit (**photo h**).

❸ Each rivet needs to be the length of the thickness of the two metals being joined plus the diameter of the wire. If the rivet is too long, it will bend; if it's too short, there won't be enough metal to create a head. Cut each rivet from a longer piece of wire as you need it (**photo i**). File the ends of the wire piece flat, even, and smooth. If you don't, the rivet head won't form properly.

❹ Work on the first two rivets simultaneously so the disk doesn't slip. Place the wire pieces in the holes with the copper back piece resting on the steel block and the rivets extending above the metal (**photo j**). (Note: this photo shows one rivet cut too short and the other too long.) If a rivet falls through, just put it back in. With the narrow end of the riveting hammer, gently tap the wire (**photo k**). (Basically, you're just letting the hammer fall against the wire.) Rotate the copper back piece as you strike the wire. After one rotation, turn the piece over and repeat on the other side. As you keep rotating and flipping the piece, the wire will begin to flatten and spread (**photo l**). When you have a good sized "mushroom" top on both sides of both rivets, switch to the flat end of the hammer. Keep hammering

MATERIALS

Note: metals are sold in sheets 6 in. wide by whatever length you order. For this project, purchase a piece of copper 3 in. x 6 in. (7.6cm x 15cm) and ask the supplier to cut it into two 3-in. pieces. (The charge is nominal and makes your work easier.) You can buy the silver as a pre-cut disk (get an extra disk as a precaution).

- 3 x 3 in. (7.6 x 7.6cm) 20-gauge copper sheet
- ½ in. (1.2cm) 24-gauge silver disk
- 1–2 ft. (30–61cm) 16-gauge copper wire
- 15 in. (38cm) 18-gauge silver wire
- 6 in. (15cm) 12-gauge silver wire
- rubber cement
- 2 glass beads, approx. 15mm and 12mm
- wet/dry sandpaper, 220, 400, and 600 grit
- Winox silver oxidizer
- fine steel wool
- beeswax
- extra-fine point Sharpie marker

Tools: jeweler's saw frame; **12–36** 4-in. saw blades, size 2/0; V-slotted bench pin and clamp; Swiss needle files, set of 6; 6-in. half-round file; roundnose pliers; diagonal wire cutters; riveting hammer; drill or hand-held motor tool; #52 and #55 drill bits; center punch or nail; steel block or hard surface to pound on

Many of the tools you need can be found at your local hardware store. Get the rest from a jewelry supply house—see "Resources," p. 56.

until the rivets hold the two metals together tightly.

❺ Drill the remaining holes and file the back to remove burrs. Sand the back to completion. Lightly file and sand the silver disk. Make sure it's perfectly sanded with no scratches—you won't be able to sand it after putting in the rivets (**photo m**). Try not to hit the back piece with the riveting hammer, or you may leave a ding. To protect a piece from light taps while hammering down a rivet, tape it with drafting tape, which doesn't stick like masking tape.

FINAL TOUCHES

❶ Use the center punch to make random indentations among the rivets (**photo n**). Then make sure that all the areas are well sanded, sanding in the same direction at all times. You need to sand the rivets aggressively with grit 220, making sure that you don't rescratch the copper portion of the brooch. Make sure there are

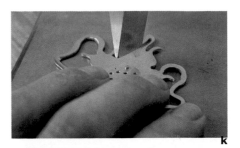

k

l

m

n

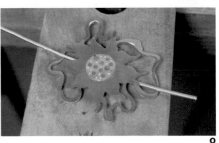

o

no sharp edges to catch on clothing.

❷ Gently bend back the metal ribbons so the 12-gauge silver wire will slide over them and under the center of the brooch. Use your fingers, since tools might mar the metal you have been working so hard to finish. Experiment until you like the look and the wire rests solidly in place (**photo o**).

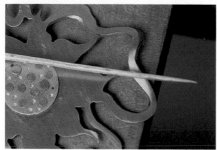

MAKING THE STICK PIN

❶ To prevent the decorative bead from falling off the end of the 12-gauge wire, make a rivet head on one end. Tape the wire to prevent scratches and place it in a vise (or grip it with a heavy pair of pliers rested against the steel block). Make sure that only a little wire extends from the vise so it won't bend while you are forming the rivet head. Since the wire is stationary, you must rotate the hammer while forming the head. Check to make sure the rivet is large enough by sliding the bead onto the wire. If it slides off, reclamp the wire in the vise and continue hammering to enlarge the rivet head.

❷ Slide the bead onto the wire to rest tightly against the rivet head and bend the wire with roundnose pliers to create decorative spirals (**photo p**). Make sure that the bead is held tightly between the rivet and the first wire curl. But don't twist the wire too tightly against the bead or the bead might break. You may use two-part epoxy or jeweler's cement for extra security and to keep the bead from rotating on the stick pin. Place the wire back in the copper shape to determine how far you want the pin to protrude beyond the piece (make sure to leave a long enough tail).

This pin mechanism is not very refined; it will destroy fine fabrics like silk. Be sure, therefore, to allow enough space for heavier fabrics when determining the arc in the pin and the bend of the copper edges.

❸ Cut the wire to the desired length and file it to a gradually tapered, sharp point with the half-round file (**photo q**). Sand the pin with all grits.

FINISHING THE SURFACES

Winox is a chemical oxidizer that colors silver and gold. It doesn't work well on copper. Like all metal colorants, it is hazardous and must be handled with care. Work in a well-ventilated area, away from children, pets, and food. Using a small amount on a cotton swab, apply it to the silver disk and rivets. (If you get any on the copper-backed piece, you'll have to sand it off.) Let the Winox dry and then gently rub off some of the oxide with fine steel wool. The more you rub, the lighter the silver will become. Repeat on the silver stick pin.

HEAT TREATING COPPER

The heat from a jeweler's torch produces wonderful colors on copper: orange turns to red, then pink and purple. You can produce a similar effect using your kitchen oven. Preheat your home oven to 400° and place the copper on a baking sheet. Heat it for about 5 minutes and remove to check the color. Keep heating until you have a color you like (**photo r**). If you overheat, the piece will turn gray or too dark. Just remove the color with steel wool and try again. The color must be sealed to prevent rubbing off with wear. Johnson's Paste Wax is a good product to use for this. Coat the piece lightly and remove the excess with a soft cloth.

MAKING THE PENDANT

This pin is an excellent way to display one or two unique beads such as the art glass beads shown on p. 49.

❶ Use roundnose pliers to make a freeform coil shape on one end of a 6-in. (15cm) piece of 18-gauge wire.

❷ String a large focal bead on the wire, securing it with glue if desired.

❸ Make another coil on the other side of the bead to hold it in place.

❹ Bring the wire through the bottom of the copper ribbon and make a few more coils and loops to balance the large bead (**photo s**).

Designed by Suzanne Stern. Contact her in care of Kalmbach Publishing at books@kalmbach.com.

Designer disks

Done completely without a torch or chemicals, this unique method of sewing with wire permanently secures components without soldering.
To pattern silver, inscribe a design into the head of a steel hammer (**photo a**, p. 54) with a Foredom Flex Shaft and a diamond bit.

The bracelet and pendant above are assembled using the same method: The elements in both are decorated with spirals, beads, and tourmalines. The earrings are coiled wire spirals.

BRACELET
The finished bracelet is 7 in. (18cm) including the clasp.

MAKE THE BASE ELEMENT
❶ Trace the template for the bracelet element (**figure 1**, p. 54) on the silver sheet with a pen or pencil. Using a bench pin and jeweler's saw, cut out the element (see "Sawing metal," p. 48).
❷ Place it on a steel bench block and strike it several times with an inscribed or smooth hammer (**photo b**, p. 54).

❸ Mark points a, b, and c (**figure 1**, p. 54) on the element. With a flex shaft or drill and a .055mm bit, drill a hole at each point (**photo c**, p. 54). Use a jeweler's file to remove burrs.
❹ Place the element in the large hole of a dapping block. With a punch and hammer, strike it two or three times (**photo d**, p. 54).
❺ File the element's edges with a metal file. If the element distorts when inscribing or dapping it, filing will reshape it.

a

b

c

d

e

f

g

h

i

j

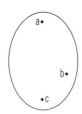

figure 1

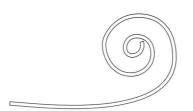

figure 2

on itself and push the length of the wire around it. As you extend the spiral, open the pliers and reposition it several times (**photo e**). Create a flat spiral the shape and size of **figure 2**.

3 Place the wire on a steel bench block. Lightly strike it a few times with the inscribed hammer.

4 If desired, use liver of sulfur and buff the spiral.

5 Make three more spirals.

JOIN THE BASE AND SPIRAL

1 Position a spiral over an element. If it extends over the edge, grasp the center with pliers and twist it smaller. Use a pen to mark the wire where it will pass through hole **b** in the element. Use chainnose pliers to bend the wire perpendicular to the spiral at that point (**photo f**).

2 Thread the long end of the spiral down though the hole (**photo g**). Snug the spiral against the base. Trim the wire to 1¼ in. (3cm).

3 With pliers, thread the end of the wire up through hole **a** (**photo h**).

4 Using chainnose pliers, flatten the wire against the back of the link (**photo i**).

5 Use roundnose pliers to form a loop with the wire tail (**photo j**).

6 Repeat steps 1–5 with the other three elements.

ADD THE BEADS

1 Cut a 4-in. (10cm) length of 26-gauge wire.

2 Starting ¼ in. (6mm) from the center, wrap it around the 16-gauge spiral several times (**photo k**).

3 Starting with a larger bead, string silver beads and tourmalines on the wire.

4 Position the wire and beads to flow along the center of the spiral (**photo l**).

5 Near point **b**, wrap the wire around the 16-gauge spiral several times to secure.

6 Repeat steps 1–5 with the other three elements.

MAKE THE SPIRAL LINK

1 Cut a 2¼-in. (6.3cm) piece of 16-gauge wire. Using **figure 3** as a template, repeat steps 2–4 of "Make the spiral."

2 Make four spiral links.

6 If desired, antique the silver with liver of sulfur according to the manufacturer's instructions. Buff as desired.

7 Make three more elements.

MAKE THE SPIRAL

After forming a spiral, sew the excess wire from its end through the element

and create a loop at one end. With painter's blue masking tape on your pliers, you won't leave marks on the wire, and the tape won't leave residue.

1 Cut a 5-in. (13cm) piece of 16-gauge wire.

2 Grip the end of the wire with roundnose pliers and begin a small loop (see "Plain loops," p. 6). Roll the loop in

k

l

m

n

ASSEMBLE THE BRACELET

Use liver of sulfur on the jump rings and clasp if used on the other components. Buff as desired.

❶ Slide a spiral link through the loop on a spiral element (**photo m**). Press the end of the link against itself so the link will not fall off. Repeat with the other elements.

❷ Open a jump ring (see "Opening and closing loops and jump rings," p. 6) and slide it through point **a** (**figure 1**) on an element (**photo n**).

❸ To join the elements, slide a spiral link on the jump ring and close the ring. Repeat steps 2 and 3 twice more.

❹ Open a jump ring and slide it through point **a** on the last element. Slide on a hook clasp and close the ring.

❺ Open the final jump ring. At the other end of the bracelet, slide it on the spiral link. Close the jump ring.

MATERIALS

Use sterling silver for all metal components

all
- assortment of sterling silver beads, 2–3mm
- 3–4mm tourmalines or pearls
- liver of sulfur, optional

bracelet
- 2¼ x 2 in. (5.7 x 5cm) 24-gauge sheet
- 20 in. (51cm) 16-gauge wire
- 4 in. (10cm) 26-gauge wire
- 5 16-gauge 6mm jump rings
- hook clasp

necklace
- 24-gauge disk, 1¼-in. (3cm) diameter
- 9 in. (23cm) 16-gauge wire
- 11 in. (28cm) 26-gauge wire
- 2-in. (5cm) head pin
- 6mm bead cap
- 6mm pearl
- sterling silver chain

earrings
- 11 in. (28cm) 16-gauge wire
- 7 in. (18cm) 26-gauge wire
- 2 earring findings with loop

Tools: chainnose and roundnose pliers, diagonal wire cutters; bench pin; jeweler's saw with size 4 or 5 blades; steel bench block; dapping block and punch; hammer; small jeweler's file; medium-sized metal file; painter's blue masking tape; pencil or pen; Foredom Flex Shaft System or Dremel tool with .055mm drill bit

Optional: buffing wheel and compound; steel hammer to inscribe; diamond bit

PENDANT

Make the pendant as you made a base element for the bracelet. Only the component size and shape change.

❶ Using the silver disk and **figure 4**, repeat steps 2–6 of "Make the base element."

❷ Cut a 9-in. (23cm) piece of 16-gauge wire and an 11-in. (28cm) piece of 26-gauge wire. Using **figure 5** as a template, repeat steps 2–4 of "Make the spiral." Repeat steps 1–5 of "Join the base and spiral," and steps 2–5 of "Add the beads."

❸ String a 6mm pearl on a head pin. Slide on a 6mm bead cap. Start a wrapped loop above the cap (see "Wrapped loops," p. 6). Slide the loop through hole **c** of **figure 4** and finish wrapping the loop.

❹ Hang the pendant on the chain using the top loop as a bail.

figure 3

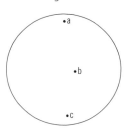

figure 4

figure 5

figure 6

EARRINGS

The earrings are 16-gauge wire spirals. Make them like a bracelet element without a base.

❶ Cut a 5½-in. (14cm) piece of 16-gauge wire. Using **figure 6** as a template, repeat steps 2–4 of "Make the spiral."

❷ Cut 7 in. of 26-gauge wire and repeat steps 2–5 of "Add the beads."

❸ Attach the loop of an earring finding to the loop above the spiral.

❹ Make another earring the mirror image of the first.

Designed by Wendy Witchner. Visit her website, wendywitchner-jewelry.com, to see more of her work.

METAL

RESOURCES

Fire Mountain Gems and Beads
One Fire Mountain Way
Grants Pass, OR 97526-2373
800-423-2319
firemountaingems.com
Supplies available: Niobium; super-fine
beading wire; tigertail beading wire;
Colourcraft wire; precious metal;
twisted wire; more

Indian Jewelers Supply Co.
601 E. Coal Ave.
Gallup, NM 87301-6005
800-545-6540
ijsinc.com
Supplies available: Nickel, brass, and
sterling wire, including decorative
varieties; silver, gold, brass, and nickel
bezel strip; sheet metal; more

Jewelry Supply
301 Derek Place
Roseville, CA 95678
916-780-9610
jewelrysupply.com
Supplies available: Gold, gold-filled,
sterling silver wire in a variety of
profiles; copper, brass, nickel, and
Artistic Wire; more

Rio Grande
7500 Bluewater Road NW
Albuquerque, NM 87121-1962
800-545-6566
riogrande.com
Supplies available: Extensive selection
of gold, silver, and platinum wire; discs;
beads; bezel tubing and sheets; more

Thunderbird Supply Company
1907 W. Historic Rte. 66
Gallup, NM 87301
800-545-7968
thunderbirdsupply.com
Supplies available: Copper, gold, gold-
filled, fine silver, silver-filled, nickel
silver, red brass, sterling and sterling
metals available in an extensive variety
of wire, sheets, bezel, tubing, solder,
discs, heishi profiles; more